PRAISE FOR GO BE BRAVE

"Leon Logothetis makes a compelling case for the importance of bravery in our lives, then lays out a series of steps for achieving this lofty aim. If you're searching for the path to your best life, the journey starts here."
—DANIEL H. PINK, #1 *NEW YORK TIMES* BESTSELLING AUTHOR OF *THE POWER OF REGRET, DRIVE,* AND *WHEN*

"This book will get you out of your head and into your heart. It's like rocket fuel for the soul. Bravery is daring to think what you have not yet thought and to dream what you have not yet dreamed, reaching beyond who you used to be. *Go Be Brave* is the road map that will take you there!"
—MIKE DOOLEY, *NEW YORK TIMES* BESTSELLING AUTHOR OF *INFINITE POSSIBILITIES*

"Leon Logothetis has spent years being a champion of kindness. Now he's spreading the gospel of bravery. This world could use a lot more of both, which is why I'm doing my part to spread his gospel."
—A.J. JACOBS, *NEW YORK TIMES* BESTSELLING AUTHOR OF *THE YEAR OF LIVING BIBLICALLY*

"The world desperately needs creative, authentic, and kind people who can solve the world's problems with curiosity and compassion. This journal truly helps mobilize the brave behavior that lives in all of us."
—HOUSTON KRAFT, COFOUNDER OF CHARACTERSTRONG AND AUTHOR OF *DEEP KINDNESS*

"*Go Be Brave* is a fun and breezy read—but don't let that fool you. This is a book that challenges reader. Read it and you'll have no choice but to go out and be brave. Leon Logothetis has precisely the message the world needs right now. As Leon makes clear, bravery takes many forms. To me, bravery begins by being unafraid to stand up for your beliefs, but also try to understand to those who believe differently."
—JONATHAN KARL, ABC NEWS CHIEF WASHINGTON CORRESPONDENT & COANCHOR OF *THE WEEK*

"An uplifting examination of self. If fearless introspection is your thing, this book is for you."
—JAMES BREAKWELL, AUTHOR OF *HOW TO BE A MAN (WHATEVER THAT MEANS)* AND @XPLODINGUNICORN

"*Go Be Brave* is a lovely and highly readable book that encourages people to live their authentic lives—and provides real and practical strategies we can all use to live our best (and bravest) lives!"
—DR. CATHERINE SANDERSON, AUTHOR OF *THE POSITIVE SHIFT*

"This book is a true gem for our generation and much needed. And it reminds us that once we find the courage to face our fears, everything changes. Great book!"
—KURTIS LEE THOMAS, AUTHOR OF *THE WORLD IS YOURS*

"*Go Be Brave* is coming into our world at an ideal time. Everything is calling us to bravery . . . bravery in how we show up, bravery in how we use our voices, bravery in our healing, bravery in our actions, bravery in our compassion. It's most definitely time to go. Be. Brave!"
—TRACY LITT, AUTHOR OF *WORTHY HUMAN* AND FOUNDER AND CEO OF THE LITT FACTOR

ALSO BY LEON LOGOTHETIS

Go Be Kind

Live, Love, Explore

The Kindness Diaries

Amazing Adventures of a Nobody

GO BE BRAVE

24¾ ADVENTURES FOR A FEARLESS, WISER, AND TRULY MAGNIFICENT LIFE

Leon Logothetis

Illustrations by Dheeraj Nanduri

BenBella Books, Inc.
Dallas, TX

BenBella

BenBella Books, Inc.
10440 N. Central Expressway
Suite 800
Dallas, TX 75231
benbellabooks.com
Send feedback to feedback@benbellabooks.com

BenBella is a federally registered trademark.

Printed in the United States of America
10 9 8 7 6 5 4 3 2 1

Library of Congress Control Number: 2022038261
ISBN 9781637742518 (print)
ISBN 9781637742525 (ebook)

Editing by Leah Wilson and Rachel Phares
Copyediting by Alyn Wallace
Proofreading by Jennifer Canzoneri and Denise Pangia
Text design and composition by Kit Sweeney
Cover design by Sarah Avinger
Cover illustration by Dheeraj Nanduri
Printed by Lake Book Manufacturing

Kami, this is for you.

DISCLAIMER:

When you read beyond this page,
everything will change.

That is a warning.

And a promise.

"SHE WHO IS BRAVE IS FREE."

—ANONYMOUS

FOREWORD

"WHEN PONDERING ON THE VASTNESS OF THE COSMOS, PLEASE KEEP IN MIND, BELOVED, THAT IT GOES EVEN FARTHER INWARD, FROM WHERE YOU NOW SIT, THAN OUTWARD.

YEAH, YOU'RE DEEP."

—THE UNIVERSE

P.S. SAVE GAS, PAPER, AND THE ILLUMINATION OF YOUR E-BOOK READER: GO WITHIN—WHERE ALL OF LIFE'S MYSTERIES APPEAR IN "PRIMARY COLORS."

It's not every day we make a friend who knows us well enough to ask questions that slide past our defenses, who shares our values, and who loves us no matter what.

Which makes today rather extraordinary.

Because starting today, Leon, through the timeless nature of the written word and the hidden, magical organization of this brilliant Universe, is that new friend for you.

Maybe that sounds like a bold claim, but I speak from experience—not only because I've known Leon for years, but because I was among the first to read this gem and to muck it up with scribbles, smiley faces, and a few tears.

Even better than having Leon as a friend, however, is becoming a friend to yourself. While working my way through this wonderful little journal, I've marveled at the wisdom his simple but pointed questions have elicited from me, revealing how brave I am and how much I deserve—and how, by seeing my own humanity, I can see the humanity in others.

As humans, we've been taught for far too long, since time immemorial, that in order to seek greater knowledge we need to search more, read more, and study more. A *lot* more. And however much we've already stretched ourselves in these pursuits, conventional wisdom demands we stretch further. But absent from such sage and well-intentioned advice has been an invitation and the guidance to look within ourselves, a place where there are truly no secrets. A place where all the knowledge and power and love we could possibly seek already reside.

As you embark upon this adventure into the sacred jungles of time and space, as you embrace the most vulnerable parts of yourself, there's nothing more debilitating than not knowing the truth. Conversely, there's nothing more empowering than discovering it. Our highest calling in life is to ask ourselves more questions, and it's everyone's right and highest responsibility to answer them—no matter how clueless we may feel at first. Life, after all, is the ultimate *unknowable*—it's where we find out who we are, how we got here, and what we can do with our time in space. And the more we begin to understand ourselves, the more we connect with our humanity, and the richer our lives become. For if you're beginning to understand that, through the law of attraction, *thoughts become things* and that you are (your) life's creator, then you're ready to understand that, as the creator of all you survey—whether your figurative lions and tigers and bears or your most outrageous dreams—you are their greater. Without you they would not exist.

Time and space are not the Harvard of reality but its kindergarten. In other words, they're the foundation of our being. Just look at how well we've already done for ourselves, individually and as a civilization, in spite of *not* knowing who we really are. Can you even imagine how much more spectacular life will become as you delve deeper and deeper into self and truth? It's the ultimate act of vulnerability. Of fearlessness. I don't think we can quite imagine all of the glory that awaits us when we tap into this bravery, which, happily, won't stop *your* inevitable march towards gaining mastery over all things. *All things.*

Of course, the certainty of your happily conquering self and of life's illusions doesn't mean your path is going to suddenly become easy. But you didn't sign up for easy. You signed up for adventure, and the telling proof lies in the challenges you've already risen above along the way. Still, if you're like me, confidently and bravely moving forward could be a lot easier than you've made it so far. *There's a sleeping giant within you that longs to awaken,* which is exactly why you've made it this far.

You hold in your hands the keys to the kingdom/ queendom of your wildest dreams. Not just because that's where the world spins, but because, I presume, you are holding this very special little journal. A journal that is as beautiful as it is potent—much like yourself. Let it be the portal into the *best version of your life.* Allow Leon to guide you back into the world of people and love. I encourage you to play full-out with its exercises so that you may sooner come to know and love yourself—it worked for me. You have nothing to lose and everything to gain. *Everything.*

Go be brave,

Mike Dooley

Author of *Notes from the Universe* and *New York Times* bestseller *Infinite Possibilities: The Art of Living Your Dreams*

A RATHER LONG DEFINITION OF WHAT IT REALLY MEANS TO BE BRAVE

(OTHERWISE CALLED THE INTRODUCTION)

When was the last time *that you were* BRAVE?

Yes, you 😊, the wonderful reader of this little journal that will most definitely change your life.

Yup, I just went all out and promised you that by reading this journal (and *doing* this journal, because there is a lot of doing in these pages) **YOUR LIFE WILL BE CHANGED.**

I'll ask it again, but a little quieter this time:

WHEN WAS THE LAST TIME *THAT YOU WERE* **BRAVE**?

Now, wait a second before you answer. I am going to surprise you—it's a good surprise, I promise, and well worth the wait ...

I am 99.9 percent sure that you were brave *today*.

You might find that hard to believe.

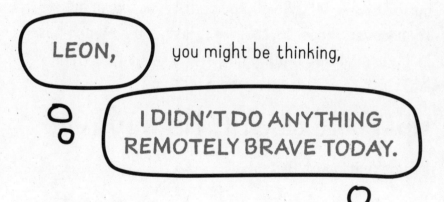

LEON, you might be thinking,

I DIDN'T DO ANYTHING REMOTELY BRAVE TODAY.

But **M A Y B E**, you're not actually sure what bravery means ...

Time for a **POP QUIZ**!

WHAT DO YOU MEAN? WE JUST GOT STARTED!

And, yes, we did—but we're not wasting any time here. We've all spent enough time reading books, listening to podcasts, trying to find the thing that will make us . . .

TRULY HAPPY.

Well, guess what? That big truth has been inside you ALL ALONG. That hidden treasure has been waiting for you to find it.

But in order to find that hidden (and sometimes buried—like really deeply buried) treasure, in order to discover those truths, we first need to learn how to be brave. But maybe not in the ways you think. So, first try to answer the question . . .

WHAT DOES BRAVERY MEAN TO YOU?

My definition of bravery is:

_____

_____

_____

_____

Great! Now, I'll offer you mine:

LEON'S (FORTY-SOMETHING YEARS IN THE MAKING) DEFINITION OF BRAVERY:

1 *Bravery* is befriending the vulnerable place at the center of our being that needs us more than anything has ever needed us before.

2 Bravery is *choosing* to reconnect to our humanity.

In other words:

BRAVERY IS ACTUALLY THE GREAT ACT OF BEING HUMAN.*

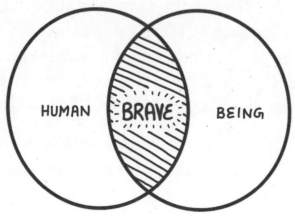

HUMAN BRAVE BEING

*Illustration Disclaimer: See that previous illustration? And the one before that? Now, wait a second before you just move on from them. Take a moment and look at them. Do you feel something? What do you feel? As you work through this journal, I ask that you pause at the illustrations, and let yourself experience them, let yourself feel them, and then keep reading once that feeling has passed. The illustrations aren't here just for decoration (though they're pretty cool—thanks Dheeraj!); they're here to help you truly *feel the feelings* that will allow you to become more fearless, wiser, and live a more magnificent life.

When I was a kid, I dreamt of being a Navy SEAL—I mean, I'm English, so this dream wasn't exactly realistic. But the point is, I wanted to be a great warrior. I had been bullied my whole childhood and I wanted to be someone that other people respected; someone who was brave, strong, even invincible—and in my mind, this described Navy SEALs, perfectly.

So, you can imagine my surprise when, years later, I was attending a spiritual retreat for depression and found myself sitting across from a real-life Navy

SEAL. And he was struggling with the same issues I was: chronic depression and anxiety.

It didn't matter that he *had been* a warrior; he was still a human being.

But what really shocked me was what the Navy SEAL shared on his last day at the retreat. He told us that in his work, he had seen what most people considered bravery out on the battlefield—where risking one's life is part of the job description—and that his fellow SEALs were certainly brave, but, as he shared, "The real bravery is what happens in here, between all of us. Because when people are sharing *who* they are, when they're *trying* to get better ... *that's* bravery."

BRAVERY means to find the place within ourselves that feels broken (sometimes in big ways, other times in small ones), a place we all have, and to give it hope. It means finding that place at the very center of our existence that we've been avoiding, but that desperately needs our attention and love. That delicate place, the one that we're so afraid to let the world see because we've been hurt there before. That place is the key to unlocking our bravery.

It is the hidden treasure within us all.
The most true and powerful source of who we are.
AND THAT PLACE is our humanness.

Bravery is *finding* <u>that</u> space; courage is *living* it.

I know what you're thinking . . .

OH, NOW YOU'RE THROWING IN BRAVERY AND COURAGE, LEON?

But they are equally important because you can't be courageous without being brave. Just as bravery is finding the vulnerable place within us, *courage* is taking the action to share it.

And when we choose bravery, when we're really, really willing to be vulnerable enough to embrace our humanness and share it with others, we can create a magnificent life from that human place. A life that is filled with wonder

AND MYSTERY
AND CREATIVITY

AND CONNECTION
AND LOVE.

And we discover that seeking the truth of who we are is actually the greatest adventure we can take. An adventure bigger than skydiving off the tallest building in the world (which would also require a trip to Dubai), more exciting than the pyramids of Mali (which outnumber those in Egypt by far), more powerful than facing your greatest fear (which we actually do every day— the question is do we also *embrace* that fear).

I'll be honest. I haven't always been so good at embracing it myself.

For a long time, I refused the adventure. I played it safe, I stayed small, I didn't face many fears, I barely even looked in the mirror. And then one day, I said ...

ENOUGH!!!!

So I set out on a journey, and what a JOURNEY it has been. I've spent the last fifteen years traveling the world, connecting with different people, cultures, and countries—I chose adventure. And in the process, I realized that I didn't need money or stuff or all the things I thought I needed to be happy.

I JUST NEEDED TO BE KIND.

In fact, I've kind of become known as **"THE KINDNESS GUY."**

It's my handle, my brand, my business. But one of the most powerful things I have learned about kindness is that being kind is the bravest and most important act each and every one of us can make.

Why, you ask? Because kindness connects us to our humanity, to that vulnerable place at the center of our being that needs us more than anything has ever needed us before.

And it's from that space we are able to move out of

FEAR,

HESITATION,

AND ISOLATION.

And instead, that vulnerable place is where we begin to live our most magnificent lives from. And when we access that humanity, that vulnerability, we find that hidden treasure ... the treasure that's been there the whole time.

Now, here's a (possibly) unfortunate **REAL-LIFE FACT:**

We live in a world where the delicate nature of our hearts and our humanity takes a back seat to how many followers or how much money or status we have.

But what if none of that material stuff truly mattered? (No, seriously, sit in that for a moment: What if none of it *truly* mattered ...)

I'm not saying you have to sell everything you own and wander the world like a monk— though if that's your thing, go wander!

I'm just saying, what if all that mattered
was that we woke up every day
and chose to stand in our HUMANITY,

to tap into who we are, like this funny,
spontaneous, brilliant, exceptionally handsome,
loving, odd English guy I know, who likes to
travel the world and talk about kindness (you
have no idea how much therapy it has taken
for me to be able to say that, even as a joke)

and go out into the world . . .

and be that person **EVERY DAY.**

The crazy, scary truth is that we can't truly be
human (or at least be in touch with our humanity)
until we tap into the deepest, most delicate parts
of ourselves and then share those parts with other
human beings.

Humans just like you! And me. (And my dog Archie!
More on him soon.)

So, I'm going to be tough on you a bit—like
a Navy SEAL, but a really kind one.

I'm going to say, **START LIVING THE LIFE YOU
WANT RIGHT NOW.** Or at the very least, by the
end of this journal.

Because here is the secret that I shouldn't share so early in this journey but I'm going to anyway because I know you're going to keep reading, and you're going to do the missions, and we're going to have a lot of fun—like so much fun, you won't even realize you're reading a twenty-something-dollar hardcover you just bought at (insert bookstore here).

The not-so-secret secret is:

EVERY TIME WE CHOOSE BRAVERY, OUR LIVES CHANGE FOR THE BETTER.

Because no matter what has happened to us in the past,

every second of every new day, we have a choice.

We can choose to play it safe, we can stay small, we can refuse to face our fears,

or we can choose the great adventure—24 ¾ of them to be precise—to
remind you of just how magnificent life (and especially YOUR life) can be.

Yes, there are 24 and ¾ adventures. And yes, I expect you to do all of them.

Curious about what exactly to expect from these adventures? Well, wait no longer . . .

THE 24 AND ¾ ADVENTURES THAT LIE AHEAD

Some of them will be inside adventures—journeys into your heart and spirit, points of reflection and understanding. They'll involve getting to meet the *you* that may have been lost for eons.

Some of them will be outside adventures— journeys in your neighborhood, in another neighborhood, in your town, or maybe even another country. They will require you to talk to strangers, and go on scavenger hunts, and, spoiler alert, find a bravery buddy.

And every time you complete an adventure, whether internal or external, you will receive the award of a lifetime (move over, Emmy, Grammy, Oscar, and Tony!): you will receive the **MAGNIFCIENT MEDAL OF BRAVERY**!

Because we don't have to run into burning buildings or become Navy SEALs to go be brave (although those are both very noble endeavors); we just have to accept the mission to connect with who we really are.

We have to go find that person, that true, inner self, like Indiana Jones seeking out a buried treasure (except with less rolling rocks and shaky bridges—though there will be bridges to cross).

Some missions will be easy; some you will be tempted not to do.

DO THEM ANYWAY.

(Please.)

Because if you picked up this journal, if you are reading these words right now—whether you are thinking that your life is great or not so great—

there was something in you that thought, "But maybe my life isn't TRULY magnificent."

And maybe it isn't.

Yet.

But it's about to be! Because by the end of this journal, you will do the one thing,

make the **ONE BIG DECISION,**

take the great big **STEP**

to leap into the most magnificent version of life, into the **GREATEST VERSION OF YOU** (also known as **GVOY!** More on that soon).

Maybe it's something you know you need to do to live a better life, or maybe you know some part of your life could be better, but you don't know how to get there yet.

Just keep reading.

It's going to be hard and scary, and it's going to be everything you have been waiting for.

Don't worry, it's not going to happen all at once—we're going to work on it together, one step at a time, starting right now ...

Because if you choose to accept these missions (which you already did since you started doing this journal),

if you actually go out and do them (which I know you will),

your life will be forever changed—like *really* changed—and not just because some random English guy is promising you that, but because **YOU ARE GOING TO FOREVER CHANGE YOUR LIFE** (I promise).

So, we are going on this adventure together, you, me, and everyone who is doing this journal.

We are all going on an expedition to discover the true human space inside of all of us ... and then we are going to start living the magnificent life that comes from that

BRAVE SPACE.

So, let me ask you again: When were you last brave?

You might have a different answer now than you did when I first asked.

Either way, that's great!

Write it here: _____

_____

What did you do? How did it make you feel? What could you do to repeat that brave act today?

Actually, I take that back. What could you do today to *make it bigger*?

I'll wait—don't worry. How can you go be brave **TODAY**?

"I can _____."

Awesome! You've just taken the **GO BE BRAVE PLEDGE**. You've made the choice to go be brave, and guess what that also means? You've made the choice to be kind, to be curious, to be deeply connected, to be adventurous, to be forgiving, to be fearless, to be in love.

To be. A legend.

Yup, I said it.

A LEGEND.

So, are you ready?

(Of course you are!)

Because I think we can all agree it's time to live the lives we have always wanted, to live the lives we deserve. It's time to reach out and say, this has been hard and scary, and I don't know how we made it through, but here we are; and it's time we stop hiding who we are and what we mean to each other. It's time to celebrate our great shared humanness. To connect and love one another with the bravery of a thousand Navy SEALs. To go out and **GO BE BRAVE**

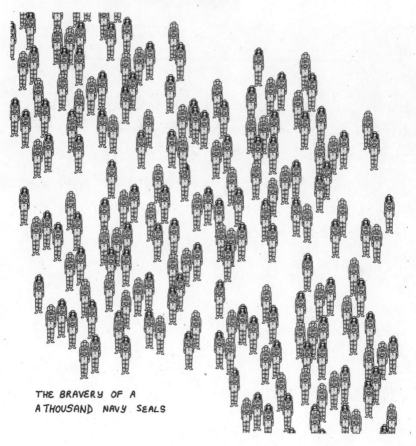

THE BRAVERY OF A
A THOUSAND NAVY SEALS

I can't wait to start the adventure with you.
Your mission has begun.

In bravery,

LEON

ADVENTURE #1

WHOOOOO ARE YOU?

How many times have you been told to

JUST BE YOURSELF?

You're about to go into a job interview ...

You're about to go on a big date
(a really, really BIG date) ...

You're about to start at a new school, or job, or meet someone important (life-changingly important), and what advice will you receive nine times out of ten?

JUST BE YOURSELF.

Easy enough, right? Hmmm, not really ...

STRUGGLING TO CHOOSE
WHICH SELF TO BE

Because being YOURSELF is in fact one of the
BRAVEST things you can do. Ever.

Being YOURSELF is the ultimate
act of <u>being human</u>.

It is finding that place inside of yourself that hasn't
been disconnected from:

THE TRUE AND DEEP KNOWLEDGE

OF **KNOWING** WHO YOU ARE

AND WHAT YOU BELIEVE IN

AND WHAT YOU CAN CREATE AND ACHIEVE AND BECOME

AND WHAT WE MEAN TO EACH OTHER.

It's where the GOLD lives.

And all those things sound really amazing, because they are.

But they're also absolutely terrifying. **#FACT**

Being yourself means that you can't hide behind anyone else—whether that's your family or your friends or your community or even your Instagram profile.

It means saying,

THIS IS ME.

I am right here,

with every incredible talent and strength and fear and flaw.

This is me,

  and I am not going to hide who I am anymore.

    I am right here, and I am going nowhere ...

Look, I get it, you're probably saying,

WHO IS THIS GUY TELLING ME THAT I HAVE TO JUST BE MYSELF?

IF IT WAS THAT EASY TO BE YOURSELF,

THEN EVERYONE ON EARTH WOULD JUST BE THEMSELVES.

You're right, and I'll be honest with you: being yourself is hard.

It's very, very hard.

It's why you are embarking on 24 and ¾ missions to figure out ...

WHO THAT PERSON IS.

Because we have been conditioned to NOT be ourselves.

To. Not. Be.

OURSELVES.

We have been conditioned to **BE WHAT OTHERS WANT US TO BE**!

So, we conform. And then we lose.

We forget that we are more than mere biological entities existing here on earth:

>We contain vast oceans of
>knowledge and understanding,

>>we contain all the stars in the universe
>>and the stardust that makes them,

>>>we contain the DNA of every
>>>human who came before us in
>>>an endless parade of human love
>>>and loss and life and death.

Yet, despite all of the magic and wonder we contain, we continue to behave the way *others* want us to behave.

So that <u>they</u> will love us.
So that <u>they</u> will **RESPECT** us.
<u>They</u>. Not us.

We tap into what some rather clever humans have called the monkey brain,

the part of us that is hardwired to believe

that if we are thrown out of the cave,

we might be eaten alive by a saber-tooth tiger.

So, we will do anything to belong.
We will become someone else,
we will ignore the vast oceans inside us,
we will hide who we truly are.

WE WILL HIDE WHO WE TRULY ARE.

I get it. More than you may ever know.

(But.)

What I also get, is that if we do not become who we are MEANT to be, our lives will NEVER be our own. They will belong to our families, our fears, our pasts, our politicians, our roles and responsibilities. We will not be OUR *SELVES*. Ever.

That sounds pretty terrible if you ask me.

A catastrophe of epic proportions.

A travesty of this opportunity to LIVE.

BUT IN ORDER TO BE OURSELVES, WE HAVE TO FIND OURSELVES.

A LITTLE STORY ABOUT A MAN NAMED LEON

I grew up being told who I was going to be and what I was going to do. Sound familiar?

For a long time, I followed in the footsteps of my family.

But I wasn't living *my* life.

FAMILY

SOCIETY

FRIENDS

I was living someone else's life, and that
life was fine for other people.

But it was heartbreaking for me.

Every day, I would wake up and go to work, and
there was no joy to any of it.

Do you know what joy feels like? When your whole
life lights up from within, when you feel so alive, it's
like the ocean is inside of you?

Yes. JOY. You can almost taste it. As I sit here
writing, I literally _can_ taste it . . .

But then there is the other feeling . . .
the one where you can't feel joy.

Where it feels like you are drowning in darkness,
the place where we cannot taste the joy
or sense the great ocean of life.

For a long time, I was drowning in darkness.

One of my first great acts of
bravery was to finally say,

"This might work for you, but it doesn't work for me."

The pain got so bad that I was forced to be brave.
Brave enough to face the pain inside me,
brave enough to face the truth inside me,
brave enough to face _myself._

To. Face. Myself.

But I also had to find the courage
to do something about it.

After a long time (probably longer
than it should have taken), I was finally
brave enough to *see* myself.

But more than that,
    I was courageous enough to finally *be* myself.

Everyone has their own mountain to climb,
but, ultimately, all mountains lead to the same
destination—the ability to be our true selves.

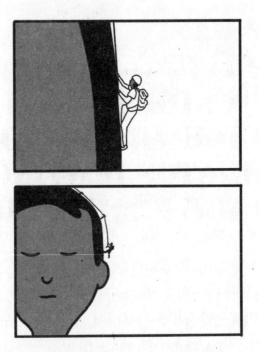

To find the gold, we can either make our way up to the top one slow step at a time,

or we can take the shortcut

and become someone else. (And I promise you, the shortcut doesn't lead anywhere fun ...)

So, there is now a very kind but stern Navy SEAL standing in front of you! That is, if this Navy SEAL was a bald Englishman. And he is saying:

STOP WASTING TIME! STOP LIVING SOMEONE ELSE'S STORY ABOUT WHO YOU ARE SUPPOSED TO BE. STOP DENYING WHO YOU REALLY ARE!*

*Disclaimer: I am, in fact, not now, nor have I ever been, nor will I ever be a Navy SEAL. But I can impersonate one quite terribly to get across Very Important Points (VIPs).

FAKE NAVY SEAL

I promise you, **I <u>PROMISE</u> YOU**,

YOU ARE MORE THAN ENOUGH! I may not know you. But I see you. And I see the hidden treasure that lives within. It is calling you, every day, whether or not you are willing to listen, and it is saying:

"GO FOR A SWIM."

"JUMP INTO THE DEEP END."

"IT'S TIME TO KNOW WHAT YOU ARE MADE OF."

It's time to recognize the humanness in you, to reconnect with what makes *you* happy. Maybe this means sharing a secret you have been holding onto.

Maybe it means admitting a fear.
Maybe it means setting a boundary.

Maybe it means telling someone, "You know what, I just can't do this anymore."

But before we can do any of these things, we need to decide where to start making changes in our lives. Where in your life are you holding onto a fear? Where in your life are you holding onto a secret? Where in your life do you need to set a boundary? Where are you not being yourself?

ROCKS AND MIRRORS

It's time to go hunting for your hidden treasure, but FIRST, we have to dig through the rocks...

So go ahead, and on each of these rocks, write:

Your fears...
Your secrets...
Your dreams...

Where do you need to set a boundary?

Where are you not being yourself?

Where are you holding yourself
back from a magnificent life?

ETCHED IN STONES

These rocks are just the beginning. As promised,
there will be lots of adventures in this journal—you
will go places and draw things and write stories and
make art and connect with people.

And also, you will be asked to do things you may not
want to do, but, as I suggested earlier,

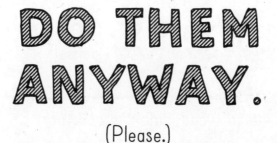

DO THEM ANYWAY.

(Please.)

Including this next one:

I want you to go to a mirror.

Right now, bring the journal, but go into your bathroom or find a mirror nearby and set your phone alarm for **FORTY SECONDS**.

Why forty seconds?

Because I want you to see who
is in front of you ...

I want you to think of everything
they have been through ...

I want you to think about every
dream they've ever had.

I want you to think about every
fear they've overcome

(or haven't overcome),

and I want you to say ...

THE BE YOUR SELF PRACTICE

Today, I, _____,
promise to stop hiding the ocean of
magnificence inside of me. I *know* who I
am. I *believe* in who I am. And I *promise*
myself and Leon (the guy in the soccer
jersey) that I will start to be **MY SELF**
every chance I have. I will practice being
MY SELF with my family and friends. I will
strive to be **MY SELF** at work and at home.
I will begin to notice the moments when
I am not being **MY SELF** and I will do one
simple thing.

I will ask myself: Who am I, right now?

WHO ARE YOU, RIGHT NOW?

_____

_____

_____

_____

I beg you. Wake up.

Face yourself.

Bravely.

And what will happen, is that
you will meet yourself on the
path and tap into your

REAL

self. After that, your
humanity will shine as brightly
as the sun, and it will extend as
deeply as the deepest ocean.

It all starts with a feeling. A spark of magic
from within. Feel it, and everything changes.

MAGNIFICENT MEDAL OF BRAVERY:

BRAVERY IS BEING YOURSELF IN A WORLD THAT ALWAYS TELLS YOU TO BE SOMEONE ELSE. TODAY, <u>I HAVE CHOSEN TO BE MYSELF</u>—IN ALL MY INCREDIBLE MAGNIFICENCE. BECAUSE I REALLY AM MY OWN GREATEST HERO (TO BE READ WITH ROCKY MUSIC PLAYING).

ADVENTURE #2

SEE WITH YOUR HEART

Close your eyes.

(I know you're reading, and I know you'll need to read on a bit first to understand what I'm asking you to do, but then, really, **CLOSE YOUR EYES.**)

WHAT DO YOU HEAR?

WHAT CAN YOU SMELL?

HOW DOES IT MAKE YOU FEEL?

We're starting easy here, really,
so I'll let you try again.

Because every adventure starts within.

It begins once we're willing to get quiet,
to truly listen,
when we begin to pay attention
to the world. And ourselves.

So, if you didn't the first time,
CLOSE YOUR EYES.

(Please.)

What does it mean to pay attention to the world?

To really, really **PAY ATTENTION**.

Now, you might be wondering,

I THOUGHT WE WERE TALKING ABOUT BRAVERY, LEON. WHAT DOES IT MATTER IF IT'S HOT OR COLD IN THE ROOM?

GREAT question . . .

It matters because bravery means we're willing to *feel* the world around us.

We're willing to go out there and meet it.
    We're willing to close our eyes and just listen . . .

Bravery requires that we step out of the busyness and to-do lists and endless chatter and madness of the news,

    and we dig deep, deep, deep
    into what we feel inside.

        But in order to feel inside, we need to
        feel what is happening all around us.

BRAVERY IS WHEN WE'RE FINALLY WILLING TO NOT JUST *SEE* BUT TO *FEEL* THE WORLD.

And that means both worlds. The inside world and the one outside of you.

QUICK SOAPBOX: It feels like everyone knows too much these days.

There is so much information at our fingertips that we've stopped asking questions, we've stopped being curious. But what if for just one day, we stopped thinking that we knew the answers, and instead started asking more questions? What if we pretended for just one day that we don't know anything at all? If we set out onto our day like a little kid, experiencing all the sights and sounds and smells and wonders of the world for the first time?

Because in order to truly be human ...

In order to connect into what makes us who we are ...

We have to be willing to SEE the world around us.

But sometimes we have to close our eyes in order to see.

Sometimes we have to embrace the dark in order to feel the light.

Sometimes not knowing is the BRAVEST thing we can do.

When I was a kid, I loved to travel.

Going to a new place meant I got to go somewhere different and *be* someone different too.

But as I got older, I realized travel wasn't about me ...

It was about seeing all the ways that people live.

It was about seeing that there are a million different paths along the human journey.

It was about having more compassion for people who didn't look or talk or act like me.

It was about fully understanding what it meant to *be* human.

And look, it's no judgment if you've spent your whole life in the same town—some people don't have the ability or the resources to travel—but you still have plenty of opportunities to discover new parts about the world around you. If you're not seeing what other people's lives and cultures look like, you're missing out on the full magnificence of life.

Because for all we know, we might only get to do this once.

I'll say it again:
WE MIGHT ONLY GET TO DO THIS ONCE.

Okay, ONE MORE TIME:

WE. MIGHT. ONLY. GET. TO. DO. THIS. ONCE.

And look, if you get another chance at life after this one, you can come back and let me know.

But for now, it's safe to say most of us only know this ONE little LIFE.

So, close your eyes again.

Imagine one place you can travel to this month, near or far.

Where is the one place you've wanted to go?

Maybe it's a bookstore in your town you've wanted to check out ...

Maybe it's an old building ...

Maybe it's a tree ...

Maybe it's booking that trip you've been planning for a while ...

Maybe it's visiting the next town over ...

Maybe it's walking out your front door and letting your curiosity lead you ...

Because you are an investigator, hot on the trail of **YOU**.

You are discovering what it *means* to be you,
what intrigues you,
what stirs you,
what makes you want to connect into the world.

Now, once you've decided where you want to travel, begin to think about what you'd like to learn there.

Is there a restaurant you should eat at?

Is there a museum you can visit?

> Even if you're not leaving your own town, is there more you can learn about people who don't look or talk or act like you?

NOW, FOR A BRIEF HISTORY LESSON: As scary as it might be to reach out to people you don't know, that's exactly how we built the world we all live in. Ten thousand years ago, it was terrifying for someone to leave their village and go to the next village. To walk in and not know if they were going to be attacked, and to ask for something like water or food or medicine. But they did it anyway.

> Travel is ingrained in our human DNA—seeing new lands is part of our human history; that's how we migrated across the world.

Don't let fear get in the way of your curiosity. Curiosity makes us wiser, and it helps us to connect into the humanness that is within us all.

And we don't have to go far to travel.

Sometimes, we just have to turn on a different

news program than the one we are watching.

Sometimes we just have to dive more deeply into someone else's life and truly feel and understand where they are coming from and what they are experiencing.

The moment you stop being curious ...
The moment you stop going out into the world ...
The moment you think you know everything ...
The moment you refuse to feel *your* inner world ...

You refuse the great adventure of life.

And you miss out on what it means to be human, to really be human; not just a follower, or a fan.

Because when we look out at the ocean, when we stare up at the sky, when we see the moon, and wonder, what is that big floating rock above us?

We can be curious

or we can just let the wonders of the world float by us.

To be curious means to always be in a **STATE OF WONDER**.

A state of marvelous disbelief about everything that surrounds us.

But (**NAVY SEAL TIME**) to lack that curiosity is to be stagnant.

And sometimes the simple act of curiosity is to QUESTION what we are being told.

To question our world.
To question our leaders.
To question our families.
To question our friends.

To be watching MSNBC and to be like, hmmm, I wonder what Fox News is saying about the exact same thing.

> Or maybe we're used to watching Fox News, and, instead, we turn on CNN.

And, lo and behold, they are saying very, very different things!

Our world is not black and white,
> our families are not black and white,
>> our partners are not black and white.
>>> Truth comes in all shades of gray.

But if we lose our curiosity, we begin to lose who we truly are.

WE BECOME MACHINES.

Do you want to be a machine?

(I mean, it might be a cool plot in a sci-fi movie, but who actually wants to be a **MACHINE**?!)

Or do you want to be a wonderfully complex creature with the capacity to wonder . . .

With the capacity to look at the sky . . .
and feel the MOON.

WHEN WAS THE LAST TIME YOU **FELT** THE MOON?

Now, I get it, you're like, Who is this crazy man telling me to FEEL the MOON? He has clearly lost his mind. And maybe I have 😊 . . .

But I am going to tell you again, and then I am going to keep telling you . . .

YOU MIGHT ONLY GET ONE CHANCE AT THIS LIFE.

And every moment is a chance
to **FEEL** <u>the</u> **MOON**,

to <u>listen</u> to the **SKY** . . .

to learn everything about the
world, even the hard parts (and
there are a lot of hard parts).

But when we think we know everything,

when we think we are *seeing* just
because we are *looking around*,

we often miss out on the big picture.

Instead, we have to learn to see with our heart.

Have you ever read *The Little Prince*?

In the story, a little boy (a prince, in fact)
goes on a trip around the Universe.

> He is looking for love,
> he is looking for home,
> he is looking for himself.

Sound familiar?

It does to me.

And on his travels, the prince meets a fox,
and the fox says to him:

"And now here is my secret, a very simple secret:
**IT IS ONLY WITH THE HEART THAT ONE CAN SEE RIGHTLY:
WHAT IS ESSENTIAL IS INVISIBLE TO THE EYE."**

So, one last time, close your eyes ... BUT FIRST!
Read the following questions and allow them to
guide you through the dark:

How can you get curious today?
How can you find the gray spaces?
How can you begin to see with your heart?

It's time to go on your mission ...

Where did you think about visiting in your town?
Is it time to book that trip?

Is it time to click to another news program?

Is it time to **FEEL THE MOON**?

Because when we realize we don't know everything, we open ourselves to the world.

We begin to wake up every day,
        with more compassion, more energy, and more
                bravery to discover
        this short
but **ENDLESSLY INTERESTING ADVENTURE**
                we call life.

But when we stay in one place, physically or mentally, it's easy to miss the big picture. Bravery, and the courage to act on that bravery, means being curious—not only living **OUTSIDE** of the box but being curious about what lies **INSIDE** all of us.

Maybe this journal should actually have been called
GO BE CURIOUS!

Because you can't be brave unless you are curious.
And you can't be curious unless you are brave.

So.

GO BE CURIOUS!*

*And remember that curiosity is an integral part of our humanness. For if we were not curious, we would still be living in a cave. Think about that one for a moment. 😊

MAGNIFICENT MEDAL OF BRAVERY:

WE CAN ONLY LEARN WHAT WE DON'T KNOW. I HAVE MOST DEFINITELY CHOSEN THE GREAT ADVENTURE OF UNKNOWING, OF RELEARNING, OF BEING CURIOUS ABOUT THIS WONDERFUL FLOATING ROCK IN THE SKY. I HAVE BEGUN TO RECOGNIZE THE BRILLIANT STARDUST IN MYSELF AND THE WORLD LOOKS COMPLETELY DIFFERENT.

ADVENTURE #3

THE TRUTH DIARY

The FIRST rule of the TRUTH DIARY is that you don't ever need to show this TRUTH DIARY to anyone.

The SECOND rule of the TRUTH DIARY is that you don't ever need to show this TRUTH DIARY to anyone.

There are some truths that we can shout from the rooftop...

I LOVE YOU!

WE DESERVE TO BE HAPPY!

KINDNESS MATTERS!

And then there are other truths—the secrets that we only whisper to ourselves ...

I'M AFRAID NO ONE WILL EVER LOVE ME.

I DON'T DESERVE TO BE HAPPY.

I'M NOT ALWAYS NICE.

(And guess what, even The Kindness Guy isn't nice sometimes—just ask my girlfriend.)

The truth diary is the place where you can share everything that you have been afraid to say out loud (and also some of the things we *do* say out loud—but maybe no one's listening). Because too often we forget what it means to tell the truth...

The whole truth...

And nothing but the truth.

SHARING THE TRUTH WITH YOURSELF

We think we're being honest in our lives, and sure, we'd pass the lie-detector test, but the biggest lies are the ones we can't detect.

The lies we tell ourselves...

About who we are,
about what we can be,
about who we love.

Even when we hurt the people we love the most sometimes.

But **BRAVERY** requires we tell ourselves **the truth**.

The. Truth.
(Finally.)

It tells us to go deep into the cave of who we really are and who we can be and who we love. It sends us into the cave with no map and a dim light and, though that can be terrifying, the deeper we go, the more we start to discover.

Because bravery isn't about **FORCING** our truth onto others. Bravery is

    feeling

        our

            own

                truth ...

And living from that **HONEST PLACE.**

Now it's your turn to get honest. Over the next three days, write in your truth diary (you'll find it at the end of this chapter). You can tear out this page and throw it away, rip it up, burn it, turn it into a paper plane when you're done. Or you can hold onto it, reminding yourself of what the truth looks like. You can start asking yourself ...

HOW DO I START LIVING THESE TRUTHS IN MY LIFE TODAY?

WHAT CHANGES DO I NEED TO MAKE IN ORDER TO LIVE MY TRUTH?

WHAT DO I NEED TO KEEP TO MYSELF? (SOMETIMES THIS IS THE BRAVEST THING WE CAN DO.)

WHAT DO I NEED TO SHOUT FROM THE ROOFTOPS? (OTHER TIMES, **THIS** IS THE BRAVEST THING WE CAN DO.)

Part of being human is the act of truly **BEING**. But how can we **BE** human, when we don't even know *who we are?*

WHO AM I?

Facing and embracing who we are can be scary work, but when we write down our truths, we are empowered. We stand up to the biggest monster in our lives: FEAR.

And we say . . .

I AM NOT GOING TO FEAR MY TRUTH.
I AM NOT GOING TO LIE TO MYSELF ANYMORE.
I AM NOT GOING TO FEAR WHO I AM.

For years, I worked a job that others expected me to work. I went to the office, I did what I was told, and I was miserable. I knew that leaving was going to break my parents' hearts (I was working in the family business, after all). But finally, someone told me to write down what I really wanted to do . . .

I wrote:

I WANT TO TRAVEL THE WORLD.

I WANT TO FALL IN LOVE.

I WANT TO BE HAPPY.

And then I wrote the truth I couldn't say . . .

I HATE MY JOB.

I HATE MY LIFE.

I DON'T KNOW IF I CAN DO THIS ANYMORE.

Once I saw my truth in black ink, I knew I couldn't deny it any longer. I had to do something about it.

Three weeks later, I quit my job and the adventure of a lifetime began.

I ask you: What does your adventure look like? What do you need to **DO** in order to **BE**?

And what truths do you need to face in order to BE truly *human*?

Look at that: if you didn't know what to write in your truth diary, I've given you a head start.

And once we start to face our truths, we begin to feel . . .

LOVED . . .
DESERVING . . .
HAPPY.

In short, we feel BRAVE!

MY TRUTH DIARY

Truth Diary Disclaimer: I don't want to give you too many hints here ... this is your chance to tell your truth, whatever that means. The truth you fear, the truth you need to share—at least with yourself—the truth you need to embrace to be loved, to feel deserving, happy. Find a quiet place you can be alone,

ALL BY MYSELF

a place you can reflect, and write down whatever truths come to mind— remember, there are no wrong answers.

MAGNIFICENT MEDAL OF BRAVERY:

TRUTH IS LIKE A DIAMOND, AND SOMETIMES THE MOST BEAUTIFUL TRUTHS ARE THE HARDEST TO FIND. I AM NOW WILLING TO BE BRUTALLY HONEST WITH MYSELF AND TO SEE MY LIFE AS IT TRULY IS AND AS IT TRULY CAN BE.

ADVENTURE
#4

IT ALL STARTS WITH COURAGE

WHAT DO YOU MEAN, LEON? I WAS JUST GETTING USED TO BRAVERY AND NOW YOU'RE GOING TO MAKE ME FIGURE OUT COURAGE?

Yep, I sure am.

Because in order to start finding those hidden treasures within ourselves,

> we need to be brave enough to
> start the journey . . .

And courageous enough to finish it.

But first, we must start by figuring out what COURAGE means to all of us. I've already given you an idea about what courage is in a very general sense, but we need to create our own definition.

That's right, this is WEBSTER'S DICTIONARY, and <u>YOU</u> ARE WEBSTER.

Which means it's time to fully embrace what BEING COURAGEOUS means to you.

For a lot of us, we think of being courageous
> as being strong,
> > as being true,
> > > as being great.

And who doesn't want to be the strongest version of themselves,
     and the truest,
          and the greatest?

We all want to be our OWN GOAT.

But what if courage wasn't about being the GREATEST OF ALL TIME...

What if courage was just about being the **GREATEST VERSION OF YOU** (so, more like GVOY than GOAT—not as catchy, but we'll work with it)?

The thing is, we can't be either one if we're not willing to do the work to GET THERE,

     and courage is what GETS US THERE.

A LITTLE STORY ABOUT A BOY NAMED LEON

When I was a little English boy, I was AFRAID of everything.

ME   FEAR

Every summer, we would go to the beach, which sounds great, right?

The only problem was, this beach had a **BIG ROCK**

that all the other kids would jump off of into the water.

But I, the little English boy, was too scared.

I would think about

WHAT IF I HIT THE BOTTOM?

WHAT IF I HIT MY HEAD ON THE ROCK?

WHAT IF THE OTHER LITTLE ENGLISH BOYS LAUGH AT ME?

Finally, one day, there was a parent at the beach who saw that I was petrified,

and they said to me, "CLOSE YOUR EYES and don't think of the scary thing that will happen.

Think of what it would mean to leap,
think of what it would mean to soar."

And though they didn't actually say this, they might as well have:

"THINK ABOUT WHAT IT MEANS TO BE COURAGEOUS, little English boy ...

Because we can't be strong and true and great
if we're living in the

WORST.
CASE.
SCENARIO.

We have to think about (and feel) what it would mean to **LEAP**,
what it would mean to **SOAR!**
So, it's time to leap."

Because that day at the beach...

The little English boy jumped and he found out that

COURAGE MEANT KNOWING THAT WE HAVE TO FALL IN ORDER TO FLY

So now, it's your turn...

Don't worry—you don't have to jump off a BIG ROCK...

But you do have to decide **WHAT COURAGE MEANS TO YOU.**

Only, not what courage means to you as you are right now.

I want you to think about the little English boy in you. Okay, fine, maybe you weren't an English boy. Maybe you were a little American person, or a little Chinese boy, or a little Bangladeshi girl.

That's right, I'm not asking YOU to tell me about courage, **I AM ASKING YOUR INNER CHILD.**

Think back to any time you were scared when you were a little kid.

Think of that kid,
        and **ASK THEM WHAT IT
        MEANS TO SOAR.**

Ask them what it means to be **COURAGEOUS.**

You can draw your definition of
courage, you can write about it
(*as though you are a little kid*),
you can draw or
write it about it
with your non-
dominant hand
(use your left
hand if you're
right-handed and
your right hand if you're left-handed). YOU CAN
APPROACH IT HOWEVER YOU WANT.

The question you must answer is: What does it take
for the **LITTLE YOU** to be
        strong
            and true
                and the GVOY (greatest version of you)?

THE LITTLE YOU DEFINITION OF COURAGE

LITTLE-ME'S IDEA OF COURAGE

Okay, got it? GREAT! Now, don't you worry.

You don't need to get out there
and start *being* courageous
(just) yet.

Remember, this is just the inside job. We have
more work to do, more adventures to go on, but
you are on your way. And guess what? YOU ARE
ALREADY STRONG, TRUE, AND THE GVOY
(we're gonna make GVOY happen!). Because you're
YOU. And that's a fact.

MAGNIFICENT MEDAL OF BRAVERY:

I HAVE THE COURAGE TO LIVE THE GREATEST VERSION OF MYSELF. I SEE (OH SO CLEARLY) MY MAGNIFICENT FUTURE AHEAD OF ME, SIMPLY WAITING FOR ME TO TAKE THE LEAP.

ADVENTURE

#5

THE GREAT OUTDOORS

A few weeks ago, I woke up really early because my dog Archie wanted to go for a walk.

(He's annoying like that ...)

Actual conversation between my dog Archie and me:

ARCHIE: DAD, IT'S TIME GET UP. IT'S TIME TO GET UP!

LEON: ARCHIE, DO YOU KNOW WHAT TIME IT IS?!

ARCHIE: YES! I ALREADY TOLD YOU. IT'S TIME TO GET UP! DO YOU SEE THE SUN RISING? DO YOU SEE THE COLORS IN THE SKY?

(I have a very smart dog.)

LEON (OPENING ONE EYE): OH WOW!

ARCHIE: COME ON, DAD! LET'S GOOOOO!!!

So, off Archie and I went into the morning cold . . .

My neighborhood was covered in fog,
and I could barely see a thing; it was like
I was in the mountains of Japan.

(I have never actually been to the mountains of
Japan, but I've seen pictures!)

The world felt absolutely at peace.
     I could hear owls.
          I could hear the rustling of leaves.
     I could hear the world. I could *feel* the world.
I felt completely at one with everything.

And in that that moment of being present with the
world, I felt more **ALIVE** than I ever had.

We can all become more alive. And it only takes a
few minutes. I'm not going to tell you to meditate—
although that's a really brave thing to do, too—no,
this great act of bravery is a lot simpler than that.

YOU JUST HAVE TO GO OUTSIDE.

Yep, that's all it takes to become a little braver.
Now, I won't have you make any big promises here.
You don't have to get up early every morning.
You don't even have to do this every day.

But I want you to stop right now and walk outside. Oh, you're outside already (even better).

Or on a plane (then look outside—I mean, is there anything more powerful than flying thousands of feet in the air through the sky whilst sitting in a metal tube??? That's totally bonkers! Think about it . . .).

Or in a car (Pull over if you can.
Spoiler alert: you can).

Oh, is it nighttime? EVEN BRAVER.

WALK OUTSIDE RIGHT NOW.

Breathe in the air.
Listen to the sounds of the world.
Feel the air around you.
See the beauty of our world—even if it's just looking up at the sky.

DID YOU DO IT?
No? That's okay.
I CAN WAIT.

Oh, good, you did it.
How did you feel?
Did it wake you up?
Did it scare you a bit?
Did it make you feel more **ALIVE?**

Because for most of our human history,

WE LIVED OUTSIDE.

For hundreds of thousands of years, nature was our home.

We have only lived inside for ten thousand of those years.

We are so connected to nature that it's coded in our DNA . . .

It is our birthright of oneness.

Yet, along with all the amazing things that come with modern society,

we have lost that connection to nature, and by losing that connection to nature,

WE HAVE LOST THE CONNECTION TO OURSELVES!

(Mic drop moment . . .)

LOSING CONNECTION TO MYSELF

YES, it really is that simple.

IF YOU ARE NOT CONNECTED TO NATURE, YOU ARE NOT CONNECTED TO YOURSELF.

And how can you find the
deepest ocean within yourself
    if you don't even know who you are?

That doesn't sound fun.
    Because it's not.

So, imagine I'm your dog Archie
and I am begging you . . .

IT'S TIME TO GET UP!
IT'S TIME TO GET UP!
DO YOU SEE THE SUN RISING?
DO YOU SEE THE
COLORS IN THE SKY?

Even Albert Einstein, best known for being a genius
physicist and doing equations on a chalkboard, once said:

LOOK DEEP INTO NATURE, AND THEN YOU WILL
UNDERSTAND EVERYTHING BETTER.

Because there is no better way to reconnect to
ourselves than to reconnect to nature.
> Nature is just a mirror of who we are.
> And we are just a mirror of nature.

And if the above statement is true, which it is
(I think 😊), then our humanity cannot be truly lived
unless we GO OUTSIDE!

Turn off the phone.
And GO OUTSIDE.

Turn off the TV.
And GO OUTSIDE.

Log off your Instagram or Twitter or TikTok.
AND GO OUTSIDE (without your phone).

Go for a walk,
      or even just look up at the sky,
            and listen to the sounds around you.

It's easy to say that **NATURE** is grand and beautiful
and worth our attention,
      but it takes **BRAVERY** to dance with it.
      Because when you dance with nature, you
      are in fact dancing with yourself . . .

What I found, out there in the mist with Archie
that morning, was that

I was standing in the purist form of my humanity.

There was no distraction,
no Instagram,
no phone calls
or text messages
or Zoom meetings or emails to return.

There were no bills to pay (thankfully),
or that dull anxiety that seems to run
through all of us, all the time.

It was just me being the same as the human beings who lived here fifty thousand years ago.
Standing in the foggy morning,
standing in the great and absolute miracle
of the great outdoors.

And there is nothing braver than that.
Nothing.

MAGNIFICENT MEDAL OF BRAVERY:

THE ANSWER TO STRESS ISN'T REST: IT'S NATURE. AND IN NATURE I FOUND THE SPACE TO CONNECT WITH THE GREAT AND QUIET PEACE OF MY HUMANITY, THE SPACE WHERE MY TRUEST SELF CAN FINALLY BE HEARD. I WENT OUT INTO THE GREAT OUTDOORS AND FOUND MY SELF IN THE SILENCE. OH, HOW BEAUTIFUL THAT SILENCE WAS . . .

ADVENTURE #6

ACCEPT LIFE . . .
ALL OF IT

So, let's talk about life.

It can be sad.

And hard.

And heartbreaking.

And absolutely worth all of it.

But I'm getting ahead of myself. Allow me to start with a story...

A SAD STORY WITH A DEEP TRUTH

After 9/11, David Letterman was asked to do the impossible: host his comedic late-night show just one week after the terrorist attack that had killed thousands of Americans.

What jokes could the comedian tell in the face of something so terrible?

He decided to tell none. Instead, he offered this ...

"THERE'S ONLY ONE REQUIREMENT OF ANY OF US, AND THAT IS TO BE COURAGEOUS. BECAUSE COURAGE, AS YOU MIGHT KNOW, DEFINES ALL OTHER HUMAN BEHAVIOR. AND I BELIEVE—BECAUSE I'VE DONE A LITTLE OF THIS MYSELF—PRETENDING TO BE COURAGEOUS IS JUST AS GOOD AS THE REAL THING."

One of the bravest things we can do is exactly what David Letterman did that night—he accepted reality as it was.

> He didn't try to laugh it away
> or not host his show.

> > > He simply showed up.

When we accept life as it is, we show up for it. And even if we don't feel courageous, we pretend, because as Dave said,

"PRETENDING TO BE COURAGEOUS IS JUST AS GOOD AS THE REAL THING."

Human beings do not accept things easily, and that's actually what's motivated us to do some pretty great things:

> We couldn't accept our hunger ...
> so we developed hunting and
> gathering (and later, pizza).

> > We couldn't accept that people
> > could die from illnesses and injury ...
> > so we invented medicine.

> > We couldn't accept that we would
> > live in the same place our whole
> > lives ... so we migrated.

We couldn't accept that life could only function on earth ... so we traveled to the moon (and if Elon Musk has anything to say about it, Mars!).

But in some ways, we've become too clever for our own good.

We have outgrown the instinct that has kept us alive for thousands of years—the instinct to always be seeking something better. Because, though there can always be something better out there, often, we fail to see

WHAT IS RIGHT **IN FRONT** OF US.

And when we get caught up in *what could be*, we refuse to accept life *as it is*, and we also refuse to accept our role in making it that way.

Accepting life ... **ALL OF IT** ... means ...

Accepting you ... **ALL OF YOU**.

Even the BAD parts. The painful parts. The shameful parts. There has never been a perfect human being. EVER. And there never will be.

(Except maybe Archie, but he's a dog, so I guess he doesn't count ... but shouldn't he?)

Our lives can be remarkable and meaningful and magnificent without ever being

PERFECT!

Do you know why?

The fake Navy SEAL is back, and he is going to tell you:

BECAUSE THAT VERSION DOESN'T EXIST.

There is no perfect version of you.

There is no perfect version of life.

We will screw up, we will make mistakes, we will be unsure of ourselves ...

Just as surely, bad things will happen, people will die, our hearts will get hurt.

LIFE IS MESSY. Very messy.

And we are messy humans living messy LI'VES.

Becoming the BEST version of yourself means accepting:

THE GOOD PARTS OF LIFE
THE GOOD PARTS OF YOU
THE HARD PARTS OF LIFE
THE HARD PARTS OF YOU
THE EASY PARTS OF LIFE

THE EASY PARTS OF YOU
THE HEARTBREAKING PARTS OF LIFE
THE HEARTBREAKING PARTS OF YOU.
ALL OF IT. ALL OF YOU.

ANOTHER RIDICULOUS STORY ABOUT LEON (ME)

I have always been a famously bad loser. Like really bad. Like the person who doesn't get picked for the team not because he can't win but because he is **SO BAD AT LOSING**.

I once played a soccer match against myself (myself!) and got so mad I lost (against myself), I punched a wall and almost broke my hand.

First, who loses a game against themselves? Second, who punches a wall because of it?

> Me. That's who.
> Because I am also an imperfect human.
> I am messy.

I've screwed up, I've made mistakes, I am unsure of myself approximately 87.7 percent of the time.

And that is a wild improvement from when I was punching walls

BECAUSE I LOST TO MYSELF.

But the problem was that I didn't know how to accept that sometimes we do our best and it is still not enough.

I also didn't know how to take responsibility when I screwed up. I didn't know how to accept my shortcomings, and I also didn't know how to celebrate my strengths. (I mean, I was eleven. But you get my point.)

ROCK PAPER SCISSORS AGAINST MYSELF

Human beings are the only animals in the world who are not okay with being themselves.

A bird is not telling his friends what a good swimmer he is when he only knows how to fly.

And a fish isn't trying to fly.

Instead, the bird becomes such a strong flyer it can fly across the world, and the fish can swim across the sea.

They make it to where they need to go in life by accepting who they are.

BY ACCEPTING LIFE AS IT IS.

I'm good at certain things but not others.

And when I own that, I can both recognize my weaknesses and also stand in my strengths.

Being brave means being willing to accept life as it is.

Bad things happen. We do bad things.

People get hurt. We hurt people.

Sometimes, people even die. As shall we.

Life doesn't always make sense, does it?

Accepting that is part of bravery. Accepting who, and what, we are inside—good and bad—is the essence of bravery.

The end (sort of).

I'll tell you right now, I know this is hard. Back when I was a little English boy who used to punch walls, if someone had told me to **ACCEPT LIFE**, I might have tried to punch another wall. Or them.

Because acceptance is hard.

There are things that happen in life that are unacceptable.

And yet, still, they exist. They have happened. We cannot erase the **TRUTH**. We cannot erase the pain that lives inside us. We can only feel it, and let it out. Safely.

And once we accept the **TRUTH**, and feel it, we can begin to change our own **BEHAVIOR**.

We can start to **HEAL**.
We can start to **WIN**.
Even if we feel **LOST**.

We stop **GETTING ANGRY**.

We stop **REFUSING TO ACCEPT REALITY**.

We stop **WANTING THINGS TO BE DIFFERENT**.

And instead, **WE STAND IN THE FLOW OF LIFE**.

Even when what has happened to us **MAKES US HURT**.

It's when we **ACCEPT THE TRUTH** that we **CAN CHANGE** our **SELVES**.

And also, **BIG MIC DROP HERE**, the world.

You might be like, Oh Leon, easy for you to say, YOU DON'T KNOW WHAT MY LIFE HAS BEEN LIKE.

I don't. I don't know what you've been through,
or how you've been hurt,
or what you have lost.
Or what emotions are bubbling up inside.

But I don't have to know what you've been through to know
that we don't have to **LET IT GO**
or **GET OVER IT**
or **FORGET ABOUT IT**
to **ACCEPT IT**. To feel it.

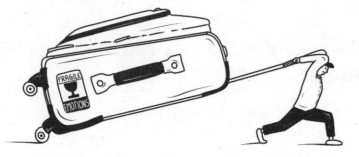

WE DON'T NEED TO LET GO

Because here is what I also know: you don't need to always be courageous. As David Letterman said, sometimes pretending is just as good.

So, let's play a little game of pretend.

Write down seven things you can't accept about life right now.

They could be about your life,
about life in general,

they could be things you don't
accept about yourself.

I'll go first:

LIST FROM LEON

1 When I think my girlfriend isn't being kind.

2 When a friend betrays me.

3 That I am not more successful than I am.

4 That I hold onto things longer than I should.

5 That I am not always living my life the way I want.

6 That some people have too much, and some people have nothing.

7 That I haven't bought an RV! Seriously, Leon—get it together!

Okay, your turn:

SEVEN THINGS I CAN'T ACCEPT ABOUT LIFE RIGHT NOW

1. _____

2. _____

3. _____

4. _____

5. _____

6. _____

7. _____

Now, pretend that you *do* accept them. Feel.
All of the feelings. Right now.

Even the hard ones.

It doesn't mean you don't work to change them.

It doesn't mean you say they're okay.

It means, in this moment, you can
see them for what they are.

MAGNIFICENT MEDAL OF BRAVERY:

I AM MAKING THE GREATEST CHOICE I
CAN MAKE IN LIFE—TO ACCEPT WHAT HAS
HAPPENED WHILE ALSO WORKING FOR
CHANGE. I CAN DO BOTH AT THE SAME
TIME, AND, IN REALIZING THAT, I AM
FINDING THE MAGIC OF HEALING.

ADVENTURE
#7

TREASURE HUNTING

Phew! That was some heavy work! (Magnús Ver Magnússon—named the world's strongest man four times—would be proud of you!)

Alright, the Navy SEAL is back
but this time, he is saying
SHAKE IT OFF!!!

We're going to go out and have some fun
(yes, with a capital F).

We're going on a **TREASURE HUNT**.

Now, if you can't leave your house for this, you're welcome to do it at home ...

But if you *can* leave your house,
then I ask you,
I beg you,
I gently push you out your front door,
and say, **IT'S TIME TO LEAVE YOUR HOUSE!**

VERY OFFICIAL RULES FOR THE VERY MUCH NOT OFFICIAL TREASURE HUNT:

Your mission, should you choose to accept it . . .

(And though I know it might sound silly or immature or like I've lost my mind, I **STRONGLY SUGGEST** you accept it):

1 Go for a walk, or bike ride, or drive, or stroll around your house (if you must).

2 Find three items that mean something to you—that could be a book, a leaf, a record, an instrument, a pen, a piece of paper, a football, a soccer ball, a doll, a rock—anything that connects you to **WHO YOU ARE**. Find three actual, physical hidden treasures that mean *something* to you.

3 Bring home whatever items you have found.

4 And finally: It's time for you to start building **YOUR TREASURE CHEST.**

Now, if you're feeling really **BRAVE**, you can build your own treasure chest. Get out an old shoebox or any kind of box; decorate it if you feel like it. Get out the paints or the magic markers, or if you're a particularly crafty sort, even a glue gun (yikes!). Have fun building your treasure chest. Remember what it was like when you were a kid, and you would chase rainbows hunting for a pot of gold. Or maybe you just did that last week.

BUT...

If you don't want to make your own box, **HAVE NO FEAR**.

Because I have made one for you.

So instead of putting your items or scribbles in a physical box, you can write them directly into the **TREASURE CHEST** you see on the next page, made and decorated especially for you (warning: no glue guns were involved in the making of this treasure chest).

Are you ready????

Over the course of the remaining adventures in this journal, you are going to see this treasure chest again—we are going to put our hidden treasures in it, and write down what they mean to us. You can use the one I provide or, again, feel free to build and create your own.

With that in mind, look at the three items you just got on your treasure hunt. What are they? What do they mean to you? Why do you treasure them?

Did you do it? Again, I'll wait.

I want to hear what you find. I want to hear about what each item means to you.

There's a very good reason for this. I promise.

In the meantime, I'll tell you about my own treasure hunt ... though it took longer than sixty minutes and it was very, very cold and pretty scary too.

LEON'S RIDICULOUS TALE OF GOING TREASURE HUNTING (IN THE COLD)

Once upon a time, I was known as one of the happiest, most outgoing guys around

(I still am, but in a better way than before).

Because I was what you call **THE LIFE OF THE PARTY**.

And I was really good at throwing parties too.

But the more people got to know me, they would find out that I was actually very sad.

Because once that party was over, I was often alone. I would sit in my empty house and wonder, *what am I missing?*

Because I didn't know what I wanted,
   I just knew that I felt lost.

      And I wanted to feel found. (A little
      bit like Waldo feels, I assume ...)

For a long time, I believed that as long as I faked being happy,

I would become it.

I thought that
by being kind and
generous and joyful,
somehow, I would
be healed.

FAKING A SMILE

I thought that
as long as I never
showed that I was
sad, the sadness
wouldn't get to me.

It worked. For a while.

But here is the thing about sadness: you can only drown in your sorrow for so long; sometimes, **YOU NEED TO JUST SWIM THROUGH IT.**

I'm not so different from a lot of people when it comes to icky feelings—and yes, icky is a technical term.

We will do anything in our powers to not feel. (Even though that is exactly where the magic is.)

We will buy things or drink or lose ourselves in relationships. (Even though that is exactly where the magic *isn't*.)

We will work ourselves to the bone, or cut ourselves off from the people we love.

We will stare at Instagram or TikTok or CNN or the hole in the wall.

We will find a million different forms of self-sabotage to stop ourselves from really connecting into the darkest and deepest parts of ourselves.

The.
Deepest.
Parts.
Of.
Ourselves.

Which, as you'll recall, is the same place we will find our hidden treasures—because those deep, dark parts of ourselves *are* our hidden treasures.

But if you keep walking through the forest, **YOU WILL EVENTUALLY FIND THE CLEARING**.

And in fact, that is exactly what I did.

I decided to **FIND ME**.

Because at that lowest point,
as I was sitting alone in my house,
wondering if I should even be here, I decided to do
what I have always done when life gets hard.

I WENT ON AN ADVENTURE.

(Because guess what? As much as travel can connect you with adventure and bravery and humanity, it can be used for escape too.)

But this time, I didn't go to any far-flung land or city teeming with people and food and exciting things to do.

I went to the wilderness (Utah specifically)...

Where I was told that I was supposed to

FIND MYSELF! by a very large man with

a bushy beard and questionable body odor,
who gave me a map and a tent and said,
rather gruffly, "Good luck with that."

Talk about a treasure hunt.

I spent ten days in nature by myself. And
I faced the sadness that, for so many
years, I had been running to avoid.

I began to look for what was missing.

I began to see where I needed to be found.

And I realized that the *one thing* that
kept me from discovering myself was
FEAR.

So the universe thought it would be funny to
teach me a really important lesson about
FEAR.

(I didn't think it was very funny at all.)

One night, I was camping by myself.

It was the middle of nowhere. Literally nowhere.
Like, Elon-on-Mars nowhere.

I hoped to find something out there—
not actual gold (although, who knows),
but the gold inside me, a gold that would

make me remember why it was so very important and precious **TO BE ALIVE.**

And though it was summer, it had gotten really cold outside once the sun went down, so when I heard a rustling outside of my tent, I wasn't just terrified to go outside—I was also freezing!

I listened to every sound, to the heavy creak of branches,

the sniffing of what I decided most decidedly was a mountain lion (or a raccoon or a mouse but look, at 3:00am when you're alone in the wilderness and you hear a strange noise, there are basically three options: lion, tiger, or bear. Oh my!),

and though I knew that mountain lions usually move through without much disruption,

I lay as still as I could, my heart beating in my ears. And then suddenly, it occurred to me that I was experiencing something extraordinary, and a voice in my head said, "Feel this."

FEEL THIS . . .

And it hit me—and I hope by now you're getting hit with it too—that time is fleeting.

It is short.

And we can either spend it staring
      at Instagram
         or TikTok
            or CNN
               or the hole in the wall.

OR WE CAN BE INSPIRED!

We can feel it.

We can feel *all* of this.

Feel the fear.

Feel the hair on your arms.

Feel your heart pumping.

Feel what it means to be human
    and alive
        and know that you won't always be
           human and alive.

And that is the most precious metal in the world.
    To know what it means to be **HUMAN**.

As soon as the sounds were gone and some
time had passed, I felt all the adrenaline
leave my system and just began to cry,

Great, heaving tears . . .

the kind the old me would have never shared about in a journal that's going to be (hopefully) read by other people.

But I lay in that tent and realized that WE ALL HAVE A CHOICE IN LIFE.

We either go out and discover what really means something to us,

OR WE BEGIN TO DIE INSIDE.

And I realized that night that I didn't want to die.

I wanted to be alive.

I'm not sure what time I fell asleep, but I woke up just as the sun was rising.

> I walked out of my tent and saw the early fire of dawn on the horizon.
>
> The air was so cold it stung my lungs, but I didn't care.
>
> I inhaled deep, heavy breaths of it, like I was drinking water.
>
> Pure. Crystal-clear. Water.
>
> I was drinking life.

I WAS DRINKING *BEING* HUMAN.

And I felt braver than I had in years.

I had found the treasure I had been seeking—
the deep and great knowing that
had been hiding inside of me.

I didn't need to fight a mountain lion
to prove that I was brave,
I just needed to cry.

I just.
NEEDED.
To cry.

I can't say that I got home and my depression was magically lifted. Unlearning old habits is hard, but you can start here. Right here, on this very page of a journal, a journal that was forged in darkness and will now hopefully become a beacon of light for you.

You can begin to unlearn all the tricks you've created to stop making yourself feel,

you can begin to move back to
your baseline humanity,

you can go out on your own scavenger hunt

and begin to find **WHAT REALLY MATTERS TO YOU.**

The author and motivational speaker Wayne Dyer once wrote:

RECAPTURE THE CHILDLIKE FEELINGS OF WIDE-EYED EXCITEMENT, SPONTANEOUS APPRECIATION, CUTTING LOOSE, AND BEING FULL OF AWE AND WONDER AT THIS MAGNIFICENT UNIVERSE.

Look at your **TREASURES** again on page 104—those three objects you found.

How do they make you **FEEL**?

Do you feel **AWE** and **WONDER**?

How do they connect you into **WHO YOU ARE?**

What other treasures can you find?

More importantly, what treasures can you begin to find *inside yourself*?

MAGNIFICENT MEDAL OF BRAVERY:

I AM ON THE BIGGEST TREASURE HUNT OF MY LIFE—THE ONE TO FIND THE MAGNIFICENCE THAT LIVES WITHIN (AND THE BEST PART IS, IT'S BEEN THERE THE WHOLE TIME).

ADVENTURE #8

TIME TO GET
VULNERABLE

For a long time, I didn't know if I
wanted to get married.

I was afraid of settling down with one person.

I was worried it wouldn't work or I
would get bored or, even worse,
they would leave.

But I had reached a point in my life where I wanted
to fall in love.

I wanted to find my person.

What I hadn't done was plan on sharing that on
national TV.

But if I've learned anything in life,
it's that being vulnerable often opens
us up to the biggest gifts.

QUICK STORY ABOUT VULNERABILITY FROM A GUY WHO IS STILL LEARNING WHAT IT MEANS TO BE VULNERABLE

A couple of years ago, I went on
the *Rachael Ray Show*,

> and Rachael asked me, "When your life is so rich
> in so many ways, what do you daydream about?"

I replied, "The truth?"

> I took a deep breath and on
> national TV, I pronounced,

"A wife."

End of Story

So here is the big secret about vulnerability,
although it's really not a secret and I strongly
suggest you shout it from the rooftops:

WHEN WE'RE VULNERABLE, WE ARE ABLE TO TRULY CONNECT WITH OTHERS.

WHEN WE'RE VULNERABLE, WE ARE ABLE TO TRULY CONNECT WITH OURSELVES.

In that moment, on *Rachael Ray,*
I stopped being on national TV.

It felt like Rachael and I were
the only people in the room . . .

     I wasn't just saying,
     "I want a wife."

I was saying,
"I've been lonely.
     I've been waiting.
I am ready to fall in love."

And she could hear that
     (even on national TV).

STOP HIDING
BEHIND A MASK

Aaaaaaaand so could the audience,
     which meant I received a number of lovely
     proposals from fans everywhere.

Though none of them panned out,
I suddenly felt different about romance.

I felt like **LOVE** was coming.

Two months later, I met my girlfriend Téa.

Because that is how vulnerability works.

When we're brave enough to

put our truths out there,
        to get honest, to feel it all,
            to show that we are just
                delicate creatures trying to find love
                    and care
                    and comfort in this world,
                        the universe hears us.

                    And it responds.

It is our birthright to connect to our vulnerability.

If we don't do that, we are missing out on what it means to be human. To *feel* like a human— not a robot.

Remember the old saying, *Sticks and stones may break my bones, but words will never hurt me?*

It's not true.

ROBOTS DON'T HAVE FEELINGS

Our words are the most powerful thing on earth
and they can be used to heal
or hurt
or share the truths in our heart.

When we are in tune with that delicate nature of our humanity, we begin to open ourselves up to others in ways we didn't even think was possible.

We begin to find love.

And not just romantic love—
though that's great, too.

So, it's time to get vulnerable. I ask you, **WHAT DO YOU WANT MOST IN YOUR LIFE?**

What is the one thing that you know is missing, as hard or as embarrassing or as scary as that truth might be to admit?

And when you think about that
thing, what stirs inside . . .

WHEN YOUR LIFE IS SO RICH IN SO MANY WAYS, WHAT DO YOU DREAM ABOUT?

Go ahead and share it here:

_____

_____

_____

_____

Now, if you're feeling really brave
    (and I think you are),
how can you share that dream with the world?

If you want to go on social media and share it there,
please tag me @TheKindnessGuy.

I will then share it to my stories
for all the world to hear.

If you'd rather just email it to me,
    you can do that too.

LEON'S SUPER-SECRET EMAIL ADDRESS THAT CAN ONLY BE FOUND IN THIS JOURNAL:

LEON@GOBEBRAVEBOOK.COM

But please don't keep your dreams
a secret any longer.

Tap into your bravery and let the
world know what you want so it
can finally provide it for you.

MAGNIFICENT MEDAL OF BRAVERY:

BRAVERY IS THE BRIDGE TO THE LIFE
I WANT: VULNERABILITY IS EVERY SINGLE
STEP ACROSS THAT BRIDGE. I AM TAKING
THE SCARY, PERILOUS STEPS TOWARDS THE
FUTURE I DESERVE, BUT I KNOW I AM NOT
ALONE—THERE ARE PEOPLE (INCLUDING THE
[NOT REAL] NAVY SEAL LEON) CHEERING
ME ON THE WHOLE WAY!

ADVENTURE
#9

THE KINDNESS DIARY

Welcome to the wild world of @theKindnessGuy. That's my Instagram handle, at least.

I didn't mean to become The Kindness Guy.

I didn't really know what kindness was all about.

And I certainly didn't know that you had to be **brave** in order to be kind.

Years ago, I found myself living the wrong life.

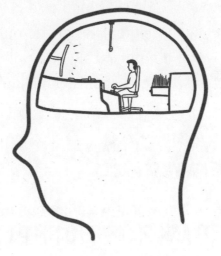

CONTROLLED BY OTHERS

I wasn't my best me.
    I wasn't even the second-best version of me.
        In fact, I didn't know who I was.

And then I watched the movie
The Motorcycle Diaries.

(Yeah, I know, a random movie on
a Tuesday changed my life.)

But it did. I saw this story of a
man traveling through South America,
    connecting with people,
        and helping them along the way.

So, if you haven't figured it out by now,

I'm kind of ... well ... **WILD** (and also
spontaneous—I definitely belong in the multiverse),
    which is why I am definitely the right guy to
    send you on wild (and spontaneous) adventures.

You see,
    I have this little TV show
    called *THE KINDNESS DIARIES.*

In it, I go around the world with no money,
AND I HAVE TO ASK PEOPLE TO HELP ME.

They can give me gas, food, or a place to stay,
BUT NO MONEY.

But along the way, I offer gifts
of kindness in return.
You see, kindness is a two-way street.
It isn't just when we give. Kindness is
also when we stand and receive.
When we aren't afraid to let
someone show up for us.
When we open ourselves up to being helped.

   And that's scary. Because when we ask for help,
      when we become vulnerable enough
      to let people show up for us,
      we also become vulnerable to being hurt.

Because throughout my travels, the hardest part
wasn't getting people to say **YES**,

   The hardest part was **ASKING
   THEM FOR HELP.**

But I found out ...
When we leave **FEAR** at home,
   and we walk out into the **WORLD**,
      a world filled with adventure,
         with the willingness to
         SHARE ourselves,
We discover something even **WILDER**:

THE WORLD SHARES
ITSELF WITH US.

Like . . . all the time.

Because here is the **WILDEST** truth of all:

Whether we realize it or not,
every minute we make the decision
    to be kind,
        to ask for kindness,
           to show up,
        we are choosing to **GO BE BRAVE**.

The FIRST rule of The Kindness Diary is that you
ASK FOR KINDNESS.

The SECOND rule of The Kindness Diary is that
you **OFFER KINDNESS.**

Ready? Let's start with the FIRST rule.

Today, you get to go out into the world and ask
someone for help.

    It could be someone you know,
    someone you've just met,
    someone you've never met.

Ask them for a simple request:
for a cup of coffee,

for help carrying something,
for directions,
for a simple act of kindness.

Or maybe a **REALLY COMPLICATED** one.

Maybe *you* need help with something **BIG**,

And you have been too (scared, nervous, upset—insert feeling here) to ask for it.

Maybe you just have to be willing to say, **HELP ME**.

And allow someone to offer you the **KIND ACT** you deserve.

(Guess what? YOU <u>DESERVE</u> KINDNESS.)

And The Kindness Guy just told you this, so it must be true!

The best part is—and here's where the SECOND rule comes in—after you receive the kind act, you get to offer kindness in return.

It could be something **BIG**, too...

Or something small.

But give back to the person who offered you KINDNESS.

Cool, right?

Now that you've practiced the FIRST rule of The Kindness Diary (asking for kindness) and the SECOND rule of The Kindness Diary (offering kindness), it's time to share ABOUT kindness.

It's time to write your **KINDNESS DIARY**.

KINDNESS DIARY*

*Kindness Diary Disclaimer: It's your kindness story now, not mine, so now you get to share about your own kindness experience. Think about how it went:

How did it feel to ask for help—were you scared? Did you almost not do it? (There have been lots of times where I didn't want to ask for help but then I would run out of gas...literally...so I had no choice.)

What did it feel like when someone helped you?

What did it feel like to help someone else?

Tell me about your adventures—were they wild and spontaneous?

Did you meet a superhero—or even a kinda-hero?

DID YOU BECOME ONE?

Kindness is one of the bravest acts we can make. It's how we connect to each other.

It's also how we connect into the best of who we are.

When I went around the world on the motorcycle,

I didn't just discover what the world could contain.

I found out what *I* contained.

I discovered just how **BRAVE** I could be.

It's time to make the **CHOICE** to

BE KIND
BE BRAVE
BE WILD
BE SPONTANEOUS

Every day.
It's really just the choice to be human.

MAGNIFICENT MEDAL OF BRAVERY:

I DON'T NEED A CAPE OR A SWORD TO BE A SUPERHERO—OR EVEN A KINDA-HERO. I JUST NEED TO BE KIND, REACHING DEEP WITHIN MYSELF TO SHARE MY TRUTH, MY FEARS, AND MY MAGNIFICENCE WITH OTHERS. I KNOW OUR CONNECTION TO EACH OTHER CAN NEVER BE BROKEN.

ADVENTURE #10

THE ART OF
FALLING IN LOVE

Okay, time for a little fun.

Have you ever fallen in love?

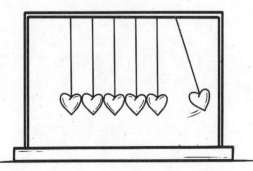

It doesn't have to be with a person.

It could be with yourself,
    or an animal,
        or maybe it describes the way you feel
        about your friends or family.

But imagine that f e e l i n g—that impossible sweet
f e e l i n g of loving something so much, your heart
could burst. Because I've been there too.

WINSTON'S STORY

One of the great loves of my life was a dog named
Winston Churchill.

Because of him, I came up with the term **WINNIE LOVE**.

I thought, *if I can love everyone the way I love that dog,*

I will be a far better person,

and if we could all love like that, we would all be far better people.

The day Winston died was one of the saddest days of my life.

A part of me felt like it was gone forever.

Because Winston made me feel unconditionally loved.

He made me feel safe and supported and cared for in ways I never had before. He also had the worst farting problem—I mean, if we can love farting dogs, we should be able to love anyone.

But after years of friendship and love and flatulence,

he was gone.

But I realized I could either try to get over him or I could stand in my grief. I could touch that broken space inside, the place we all have, and like Winnie showed me, I could find the hidden treasures that were waiting

for me on the other side of heartbreak.
I just had to be brave enough to do it.

So, think about the great loves of your life—
the people or animals who made you feel safe
and supported and cared for in ways you hadn't
experienced before. Who have you loved? Only list
five people/animals—but make them your top five:

1. _____

2. _____

3. _____

4. _____

5. _____

Okay, great.

Now, take a look back at your list,
and, for each person (or animal),
think about how they made you feel.

Sit in the feeling.

Put the journal down.
And sit.
With the feeling.
For sixty-five seconds.
Yes, sixty-five.

(I am counting . . .)

Because when we are brave enough to fall in love, it means we are also brave enough to go through pain.

To feel that
      dark
            and empty space
that says nothing will ever be okay again.

And still know that we're going to be okay.

Because **LOVE** is always there, but just like with hidden treasure, we need to be able to find it.

SO, LET'S PULL OUT OUR
TREASURE CHEST AGAIN.

In your treasure chest on the next page, write down the names of the people (or animals) you love (because we never stop loving) and how they made you FEEL.

How do (or did) they make you feel ...
Supported?
    Safe?
        Understood?

Like the farting dog you love so much also happens to be your best friend?

These feelings are your hidden treasures.

Now, who on that list can you offer more **LOVE** to today? Is it a friend, or your mom, or a grandparent, or your girlfriend, or your boyfriend?

Is it your dog?

What can you begin to do to fall in love with that person (or dog) a little more every day?

Recently, my girlfriend told me, "Leon ...

You are responsible for treating me well because I have given you my heart."

(No pressure.)

Love is the ultimate act of bravery.

Whether it's a dog or a cat
or a horse or a person or yourself,
when we fall in love, we risk
getting our hearts squashed.

But when we **GIVE LOVE**, we find out just how magical it can be.

Love can save.
It can heal.

It can make us feel alive and at one with the world.

But love also has the power to crush us,
   to break us,
      to make us believe we will never be whole again.

Giving and receiving love is the
ultimate act of bravery.

BE AN ANTENNA OF LOVE

Who can you offer MORE LOVE to in your life?

Write their name here:

What small act can you do,
every day/every week/every month,
to demonstrate to them that

you **ARE THERE**,

you **LOVE THEM**,

and you are **BRAVE** enough

to show them that **YOU CARE**.

After Winnie died, I kept waiting to feel better.

But then I realized that the love I had
for Winnie was worth the loss.

BECAUSE THE LOVE IS ALWAYS WORTH THE LOSS.

Finally, last year, I decided it was time
to get a new dog...
and I found **ARCHIE**.

But what I also found
is that the more
LOVE I have
given Archie,
the less I miss Winston.

UFF ♥

WOOF!

I WOOF YOU

I still remember him
and love him,

    but falling in love again offers
    us the **OPPORTUNITY**

to see that we can **LOSE LOVE** and **FIND LOVE**
and **LOSE LOVE** and

FIND LOVE AGAIN.

When I met Téa, I felt the same way.
    I was scared.
        I had been hurt.

I didn't know if I was **BRAVE ENOUGH**
to fall in love again.

But when we open ourselves up to the pain
    and loss
and absolute alive-ness that love offers all of us,
we fall in love with the world.

And each other.

MAGNIFICENT MEDAL OF BRAVERY:

THEY CALL IT FALLING IN LOVE BECAUSE WE DON'T USUALLY REALIZE IT'S HAPPENING UNTIL WE'RE IN IT. BUT I NOW HAVE THE CHANCE TO WALK THROUGH LOVE, TO STAND UP FOR IT, TO REMEMBER THAT EVERY DAY IS AN OPPORTUNITY TO GO BE LOVE. I AM ON MY WAY . . .

ADVENTURE #11

FIND SOMETHING
BIGGER THAN YOU

The other day, a friend asked me what I wanted to do with my life . . .

I was confused—I mean, clearly I know what I AM DOING WITH MY LIFE, THANK YOU VERY MUCH.

But then she asked again, "NO, Leon,

WHAT DO YOU REALLY WANT TO DO?"

And I'll be honest, I didn't know what to say . . .

For a long time, I had a list of things that I wanted to do—
    and some of them are kind of embarrassing.

Sure, I wanted to travel.
    And I wanted to write.
        But I also wanted to be on TV.
            I wanted to be famous.

When I was a kid, I saw this movie with this guy on a motorcycle and this gorgeous woman on the back, and I was like, *I want to be that guy.* (Spoiler alert:

The movie was *Top Gun*. The guy was Tom Cruise.)

And I *got* to be that guy. (I mean, not Tom Cruise, because that *would be* a **PLOT TWIST**, but the guy on the motorcycle.)

I traveled the world, and I wrote the books, and I got the Netflix show. I became famous—kind of—and I've ridden motorcycles, often alone, but sometimes with women, too.

But when I heard that question from my friend,

"WHAT DO YOU REALLY WANT TO DO?"

I realized I had no answer.

I explained to my friend that I have done everything I wanted to do,

and now I <u>don't</u> know what to do.

Because I no longer want to do any of the things that society,

or social media,

or even movies from the 1980s

tell me are important.

THINGS SOCIETY WANTS
ME TO DO

Because what I found as I achieved the goals I'd set
for myself was that though the books

and the TV shows are cool,

they don't bring true happiness.

And even though the motorcycle is fun, it's also
incredibly, incredibly exhausting.

>   My friend laughed and said, "I guess it's
>   time for you to have children then?"

"I've been wondering if that's
what's missing," I told her.

And then she explained that it wasn't
just about having children.

The point was to find something
BIGGER than yourself.

"In a way," she shared, "having
kids is really a cheat.
Because every day, you are
forced to get outside of yourself.
But you don't have to have kids to find that,
you just have to find something bigger than you."

It isn't easy handing over our lives to something
bigger than ourselves because, ultimately,
to do that, we must also give up control.

Control. The master addiction.
(I stole this from a very wise man by the way . . .)

But in order to be brave, we must
learn to be okay with NOT KNOWING,
We have to *get out of our selves*—which is
really just another way of saying

YOUR EGO IS NOT YOUR AMIGO.

Don't worry—I'm not telling you that you have to have children anytime soon.

But rather that we all have to find
things **BIGGER** than ourselves
in order to finally get **free** from the fears
and the boredom
and selfishness that stop us from being truly human.

Because there are hard parts to being human too.

There are nights where we might
wish that the day won't come

and days that feel like **THEY WILL NEVER END.**

But when we **FIND SOMETHING**
to believe in,

when we begin to see **THERE IS SOMETHING**
BIGGER THAN US,

we are reminded that we are **NEVER ALONE.**

That there is always a reason
to breathe,
to believe,
to *be.*

YOU JUST HAVE TO FIND YOUR REASON.

But how do we do that?

We all have to find our OWN WAY (and don't worry, we'll get to that part),

but I'll share mine . . .

LEON'S STORY OF FINDING SOMETHING BIGGER THAN HIMSELF

It was 7:58 in the morning and I was still in bed. Which isn't normally such a bad thing except that on this particular day at 8 am, I had promised to do a Q&A on Zoom for a group of high school kids.

They wanted to hear from The Kindness Guy.

Or at least their teacher wanted them to hear from me . . .
But truth be told, *I* didn't want to hear from me.

I was at a low point.

Very low.

And I had two minutes to make a decision.

Was I going to cancel at the very last minute and make up some fake story about how I was sick? And who hasn't pretended they were sick to get out of something? I mean, I'm pretty sure that's another part of being **HUMAN**.

Or was I going to stumble out of bed, and maybe, just maybe, touch a kid's life?

What

was

I

going

to

do?

<u>Then I remembered.</u>

When I was a sixteen-year-old kid, I walked into an auditorium and heard a lady give a talk that changed my life. She told the story of how her son had died in the Black Hawk Down incident in Somalia in 1993.

Her son was a man named Dan Eldon. He wasn't a soldier; he was a photographer.

But he put his life at risk because he believed that the **STORY** was the most important thing. The story was bigger than himself.

And that story was how he made a difference.

He was being driven by
a power **FAR GREATER** than himself.
The power of bringing the truth to light.

He risked his life,
     not to do battle as a soldier,
          but to share with the world
               what it means to be **HUMAN**.

He risked (and lost) his life in order to honor
     something bigger than himself:

HISTORY.

I never forgot that story. Never.

And so, years later, as I tried to summon
the motivation to get out of bed, and it felt
like the best I could do was concoct rather
ludicrous ways to skip out on high school
students, I remembered that lady.

I remembered Dan Eldon.

I remembered that I am not the
     center of the universe
(and, super top-secret secret: neither are you).

To truly connect to the **POWER** that lives
     within **EACH OF US**,
we must **FORGET** ourselves (at times . . .).

And we must **LIVE** from a place where **POWERS** far greater than we are guide us.

Because if we don't,

we will **NEVER** truly feel the electricity of our humanity flow

within our cells,
within our lives,
or between each other.

Being human means being **BRAVE** enough to look so deep into the reflection in the mirror,

we see beyond it,

to the space where we all exist.

To the place where we see **EACH OTHER**.

So, I got out of bed, gave the Q&A, and hopefully had a sliver of the impact on someone that Dan Eldon's mother had on me so many years before...

We cannot create a magnificent life, we cannot heal, we cannot even get out of bed some days if we don't find something **GREATER** than ourselves...

For some, it's being of service;

for some, it's God (whatever that
word might mean to you);

for some, it's the people they love;

for some, it's the nature around them.

For some, it's the absolute miracle
of *getting* to wake up,

and getting to breathe through another day,

getting to believe in another day,

getting to share our stories about
what it means to be ALIVE.

WHAT IS YOUR SOMETHING **BIGGER**?

Of course, it can be more than one thing.
   It can be all the things I mentioned,
      and a million more.

But for this adventure, list just one...

   And then it's time to connect to it,
      whether it's being of service, or being with
      your God, or being in nature, or being
      with the people you love, or being with
      your family...

Or just **BEING.**

Spend thirty minutes today
connected into that source.

Disconnect from your fears
and boredom
and selfishness,

and reconnect into the place that makes you feel
ALIVE.

That makes you feel deeply
HUMAN.

Because when we get trapped on the island of
ourselves—population: one—we lose sight of what it
means to be part of the human family.

Gandhi himself once said:

"THE BEST WAY TO FIND YOURSELF IS TO LOSE YOURSELF IN THE SERVICE OF OTHERS."

Because when we connect into things that are bigger
than ourselves,
we are reminded that we are not the center
of the universe.
(How could we have ever thought we were?)

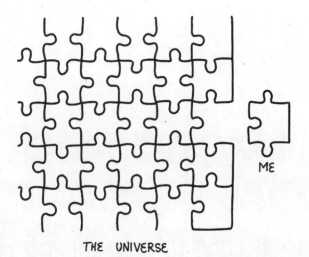

THE UNIVERSE

BECOMING A PART OF
SOMETHING BIGGER

But we are a very important part.

And when we connect into others,

we connect into the truest
versions of ourselves.

We begin to see just how magnificent **LIFE** can be.

MAGNIFICENT MEDAL OF BRAVERY:

THE MORE I GIVE UP CONTROL, THE MORE I CAN FINALLY GET OUT OF FEAR. AND THE OPPOSITE OF FEAR ISN'T ACTUALLY BRAVERY: IT'S FREEDOM. WHEN I GET OUT OF FEAR, I FINALLY HAVE THE FREEDOM TO BE MYSELF. I AM FREEING MYSELF FROM FEAR!

ADVENTURE #12

GET MAD

I have a little secret for you. (Another one.)

Like a super-duper-luper little secret for you.

Are you listening?

Can you lean in a little closer?

Okay, that's good.

Here it goes:

YOUR ANGER IS PART OF WHO YOU ARE.

In fact, I would say that anger is one of the most important parts of being human.

Of being alive.

Anger is evidence that **WE CARE**.

But for some reason, we're all taught that we shouldn't get angry.

But WHY?

Why are we scared of *our own anger?*

In fact, why are we scared of *other people's anger?*
WHY ARE WE SO SCARED OF ANGER?

(I'm asking. I honestly don't know.) Because
humans get angry.
Even animals get angry.

We get **angry** when we think we are going to lose

something we **care about** or when we **don't think** we are going to **get** something we **care about.**

And guess what? Anger is just fear turned INSIDE OUT.

And it takes BRAVERY to get angry, to say,

"Hey, this isn't right!"

"Stop, you're doing something wrong!"

"Look, I am not going to be treated that way!"

We have every right to be angry . . .

The question is, are we willing to speak UP? To speak our TRUTH.

Most of us, unfortunately, are not.

<u>Because we have been conditioned to believe that our anger is bad.</u>

And don't get me wrong, the effects of our anger can sometimes be very bad.

But as long you as you let out your anger in a safe place, and share your pain, you will realize that it takes BRAVERY to be angry—but also that **IT TAKES ANGER TO BE BRAVE**.

Because guess what?

We all have things in our lives that we can be ANGRY about,

that we *should* be ANGRY about.

And we are ALLOWED to be angry.

A lot of us get scared that anger leads to violence . . .

But people only get violent when they don't know how to safely share their anger.

THE FIVE RULES OF ANGER

1 Anger is not about hurting people.

2 Anger is not about being mean.

3 Anger is not about being cruel.

4 Anger is not about being rude.

5 Anger is about **BEING HUMAN.** (In fact, it's like the first rule of being human: you have to get angry sometimes. And if you don't get angry ever, then I'm really scared, because you must be a cyborg already!)

Because anger has driven so much of what makes humans amazing . . .
> It has helped us to invent new technologies, to make advances in science and society.

It has helped to make us freer,
> more equal,
>> more empowered.

ANGER HAS BEEN THE FUEL FOR SO MUCH BEAUTY IN THIS WORLD.

And yet we are <u>terrified</u> of it.

But what if we just had to learn
how to use it better?

A LITTLE STORY FROM A MAXIMUM-SECURITY PRISON

I give speeches in many places—
high schools and colleges,
     corporate conferences and personal
     development conventions.

But I also give speeches in maximum security prisons.

     And sadly, but not surprisingly, there
     are some angry people in prison.

Sometimes it's their anger that
     has landed them in prison,
but usually, more often, it's their life experiences
that *made* them angry,
     growing up in pain and poverty and trauma,
          and the anger just had nowhere to go.

And that doesn't mean that people don't do bad

things, but many people who *do* bad things have also been hurt themselves.

And when we're hurt, we can get angry . . .
We get angry at what we lost
or what we never had.

On one of my trips to prison, I met with a group of inmates. I didn't know why they were there, but I could feel their hopelessness, their boredom, their quiet anger at living a life that they know could have been different. I talked about

ANGER and FEAR and KINDNESS.

And how *we all have a gift.* **WE ALL HAVE HIDDEN TREASURES INSIDE OF US.**

And I asked if anyone wanted to come
up and share about THEIR GIFTS.

This guy raised his hand, and honestly, I regretted the invitation. He was BIG, like twice my size BIG. He hadn't smiled the whole time. In fact, he kind of looked like he hated me.

But then he walked up to the stage,
he looked out at his fellow prisoners,
and after a moment of uneasy silence
he took in a deep breath,
and he began to rap.

The words that poured out of him were some of
the most powerful truths I'd ever heard...
    About pain.
        About rage.
            About loss.

His whole face lit up and the room stood still.

I didn't know this man's story, but as he began to
share his truths...
    We all connected to his pain,
        his rage,
           his loss.

In that moment, we all saw a glimpse
of what it was like to live his life,
    and we became connected to him.

What if the key to our humanity
    was our pain?

What if the key to our freedom
    was our truth?

WHAT IF?

Because often the best art comes from our truth,
    our pain,
        our rage,
           our loss.

So don't be afraid to sit in your anger,
    but find a way to channel it
        so that it not only helps you to heal,
    it helps you to be heard.

GET MAD.

Great, Leon, I'm sure you're thinking. **But how?**

I mean, I did tell you about punching the wall after losing a game of soccer to myself, but I strongly **DO NOT** recommend that.

Instead, your friendly (and 100 percent fake) Navy SEAL is back. He is inviting you up on stage, and he is telling you:

YOUR <u>ANGER</u> IS ONE OF YOUR GREATEST GIFTS.

It is the fire in your belly.
It is the proof of your loss.

You can keep hiding it or letting it come out in all the **WRONG** ways ...
    Or you can finally let it out the **BRAVE** way.

It's time to find your ANGER and see it for the HIDDEN TREASURE it is.

It's time to go back to your **TREASURE CHEST.**

It's time for you to write your own truths, your own song or rap or story or poem about whatever you're angry about.

No one has to see it or hear it.

But channel that **RAGE** into words.

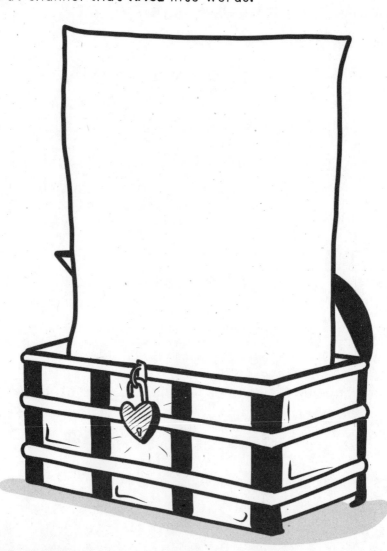

If you feel brave enough, you can post your letter or read it out loud.

You can go in the bathroom and turn on the shower, you can do it alone in your car,
you can make a TikTok or Reels out of it
and tag me @TheKindnessGuy.

Or, if you want to keep it more private, you can DM me at @thekindnessguy or email it to me at Leon@GoBeBraveBook.com.

Or you can just **LEAVE IT IN YOUR TREASURE CHEST**.

Because your anger is a very
important tool when you're
working to build a magnificent life.

But either way, get mad,
and then share your anger;
find an outlet to your pain.
To your rage.

Because we hurt each other when we don't let the anger out, when we allow it to build
and build without a productive outlet.

If you don't share your anger, it will consume you.
Because in order to control your ANGER,
you have to make friends with it. You MUST

speak to it. You must accept it. You must be BRAVE enough to share it in a way that doesn't hurt others, but funnels that anger into the TRUTHS you deserve to share.

MAKING FRIENDS WITH
YOUR ANGRY SELF

And I am sure there are many, many truths you deserve to share.

Because you are a **HUMAN BEING**.
> We lose things we love,
>> we don't get things we want,
>>> and often, the biggest thing
>>>> is that we want the world to change.

And what better way to harness our anger, our bravery, than to share our truths with the world?

MAGNIFICENT MEDAL OF BRAVERY:

WHEN I DIG DEEP DOWN UNDERNEATH MY ANGER, I FIND THE REAL SOURCES—THE FEARS, THE ABANDONMENTS, THE TRAUMAS, AND THE PAINS—THAT DRIVE ALL RAGE. I AM NOW DEEP CLEANING OLD WOUNDS, AND DISCOVERING THAT ANGER IS ACTUALLY JUST ONE WAY WE CAN HEAL. I GOT MAD TODAY! AND THAT'S A GOOD THING ☺.

A BRIEF
INTERMISSION

The kind (English) Navy SEAL has
returned . . . yet again.

And he's not mad because he is quite literally
the nicest Navy SEAL ever because he never
actually went to boot camp and he doesn't
even know how to do that many pushups—

> but he does know how to go on a bunch of
> wild (and spontaneous) adventures . . .

> In order to connect to other people,
to feel their pain and loneliness and fear,
> in order to feel alive,
> > in order to live a magnificent
> > life (a lot of the time).

And he is going to say this in the nicest
way possible, truly . . .
> with a proper English accent
> > and even a cup of tea . . .

Because we're now at the point of the journal where we can't keep talking about that **MAGNIFICENT LIFE**.

WE HAVE TO GET OUT THERE AND START CREATING IT. IT'S TIME. YES, I AM TALKING TO YOU.

YOU, RIGHT THERE 😊

Here we are, twelve adventures in.

We've done some hard stuff,
        some easy stuff,
some painful and wild and fun and I hope totally life-transforming stuff.

BUT NOW WE'RE ABOUT TO PUT OURSELVES OUT THERE.

Now, we're going to 100 percent leave the comforts of our homes—no seriously, get up, because

WE ARE GOING PLACES!!

We're going to put the "go" in
GO BE BRAVE.

And as you are going to soon find,
WE CANNOT DO THAT ALONE
(oh yes, you were wondering when we'd
meet this BRAVERY BUDDY from
the introduction, weren't you?).

Like I said earlier,
    there are some missions
    you will be tempted not to do.

You will think they're too hard...
    or wild...
        or downright silly.

But as your super-friendly Navy SEAL who does
not do pushups,

    but who *does* know how to make
    a proper pot of tea,

I have to tell you that...

It won't matter what book you buy...
    Or what podcast you listen to...
        Or which person you follow on Instagram.

You will not begin to live your magnificent life
unless you are willing to do the **HARD THINGS**,

the **WILD THINGS**,

the **SILLY THINGS**.

But if you're willing to accept the **MISSION,**
to go out there and **GO BE BRAVE,**
to connect with **HUMANITY,**
to get OUTSIDE of **YOURSELF** ...

In order to go more DEEPLY inside ...

Well, then, you are ready for the second half of this GREAT adventure.

If you're not ready, I wouldn't bother reading any further.

Truly. It's okay.

You can go ahead and close this journal, sell it on eBay, and take yourself to dinner on the profits—just don't get too excited; used books on eBay don't sell like they used to.

But ...
If you are ready to **CHANGE EVERYTHING,**
let's keep going!

ADVENTURE #13

FIND YOUR FABRIC

We are hardwired to be in community with each other.

From the moment we're born, we need *others* to survive.

We need *others* in order to eat, in order to stay warm, in order to be protected from predators.

We need **TOUCH** to survive.

We need physical, emotional, and neurological support

FRIENDSHIP IS THE FABRIC OF LIFE

in order to grow into independent, compassionate, and resilient humans.

A QUICK SCIENCE LESSON (FROM AN ENGLISHMAN WHO ONCE GOT 18 PERCENT ON A CHEMISTRY EXAM, SO HE'S NOT SURE HOW MUCH YOU SHOULD LISTEN TO WHAT HE IS ABOUT TO SAY, BUT THAT'S JUST ONE REASON THIS ISN'T A SCIENCE TEXTBOOK!)

On a neurological level, we are always interacting with each other. Our neurons are constantly mirroring one another, creating a literal fabric between humans. We model our behaviors, experiences, and how we engage with the world based on the other people in our world.

There is no such thing as a self-made person.

Everyone has had at least one person behind them
(and probably many)—
    a parent, a partner, a teacher,
        a mentor, a friend, a dog—
helping them to weave the fabric of their dreams,
    their inspirations,
        their personality,
    their beliefs,
their being.

The stronger the community around us,
    the stronger our neurobiology,
        which leads to more compassion,
            more resiliency,

WE'RE ALL IN THIS TOGETHER

            and, not surprisingly, more
            humanity in our experiences
            of life.

You see, community leads
to bravery.

But also, bravery leads to
community.

The thing is, your community
isn't always the same one you
grew up in,
    or the one where you
    think you should live.

You can find your community anywhere. You can create your own fabric.

And when we find our people,
the wildest thing is that
we find ourselves.

We see all our best parts mirrored in them.

In fact, **WE SEE WHO WE ARE.**
We see why others like us
and value us
and accept us.

Because being brave means showing people
who we really are
and not being afraid when the
whole world doesn't love us back.

AND GUESS WHAT?

The whole world doesn't have to love you.

JUST THE PEOPLE YOU WANT IN YOUR WORLD.

And you have a lot of wonderful
people in your world.
But before we can show up for our community,

WE NEED TO FIND OUR FABRIC.

ANOTHER TOTALLY FUN-WITH-A-CAPITAL-F TREASURE HUNT

In order to weave our fabric, we need to first determine what kind of thread is going to make the strongest bond. As we begin to identify (or even begin to build) our community, we need to find the people we want in it— the threads that will make up our fabric.

That's right, time to pull out your treasure chest and begin thinking about who you have in your neighborhood that:

SHOWS UP WHENEVER YOU NEED HELP.

MAKES YOU FEEL BETTER ABOUT YOURSELF.

MAKES YOU WANT TO BE A BETTER PERSON.

It could be the same person for a couple of categories. There might be multiple people for each one. It could be people you know IRL—or it could even include your social media friends.

Even if it's just one name, who is your strongest thread, and **WHAT DO THEY BRING TO YOUR WORLD**?

It's time to add to your treasure chest! Write down (either down below or on a separate piece of paper) the names of people who make up your fabric. Your neighborhood. Your community.

And now, the moment we've all been waiting for:
IT'S TIME TO FIND YOUR BRAVERY BUDDY.

Take a look at those names in your treasure chest. Is there someone in there who you would like to invite on this bravery adventure with you?

Or maybe even more importantly . . .

Is there someone on the list who needs to learn a little bit more about what it means to
GO BE BRAVE?

Maybe they're struggling with **CRIPPLING FEAR**.

Maybe they're struggling to **CONNECT** (to themselves or others).

Or maybe they're struggling to live their most **MAGNIFICENT LIFE**? (Who isn't? Well, maybe the Dalai Lama isn't, but I bet you even the Dalai Lama has bad days.)

Whatever the case may be, boy do we have an adventure for them!

Can you ask this person if they would want to work through the journal, too?

Or even just be there to talk about your own adventures?

In other words, would they be willing to be your **BRAVERY BUDDY**?

They'd be like a living treasure chest,
    holding your lessons
        and secrets,
            and reflecting your magnificence,
            showing you just exactly who
            you can be, who you are.

But also, you would be inviting them to find their own mission. You would be *their* treasure chest, supporting them through their own journey.

    Who could you call to be your **BRAVERY BUDDY**?

(You can even email me at
Leon@GoBeBraveBook.com, and
who knows? Maybe, just maybe, we
will hit it off, and we can be each
other's Bravery Buddy...)

Identifying your Bravery Buddy might help you
realize just how rich your fabric already is ... and
it might inspire you to make it even richer. As
you and your Bravery Buddy work through your
journey, consider ...

How can you begin to build community?
    How can you begin to connect into love?
How can you practice the great act of being human?

Because connecting with others to build a
community is one of the bravest things we can do.

LOVING CIRCLE OF FRIENDS

When we show others who we really are,
we don't have to worry about
whether we're smart enough,
or cool enough,
or good looking enough,
because we will have found our people.

And our people are there for us no matter what.

Because having people we can count on
is more valuable than gold.
It's rarer than diamonds.

It's more magical than any crystal or ruby or
sparkling gem at the bottom of the sea.

Our people are our treasures.

So, look at your names again.

How can you start treasuring them more **TODAY**?
How can we honor those friendships and
family members and the people we
can call just because?

How can we say,

"THANK YOU FOR BEING MY COMMUNITY,

THANK YOU FOR CONNECTING ME TO LOVE,

THANK YOU FOR REMINDING ME OF THE GREAT ACT OF *BEING HUMAN*."

MAGNIFICENT
MEDAL OF BRAVERY:

HOME IS IN EACH OTHER. IT ALWAYS HAS BEEN. WHEN I FIND MY PEOPLE, MY FABRIC, I DISCOVER THAT THERE IS NOTHING I CANNOT ACHIEVE. THERE IS NOTHING I CANNOT HEAL. AND MY BRAVERY BUDDY (INCLUDING LEON) IS HERE FOR ALL OF IT!

ADVENTURE
#14

BRAVERY IS
SAYING YES

So, a few years ago, I found myself in a bookstore.

All of a sudden, a book fell off the shelf. It literally fell off the shelf.

I picked it up and opened it to a random page, and I read these words,

"Reveal God to me and I will follow you anywhere."

It came from the classic book, Paramahansa Yogananda's *Autobiography of a Yogi*.

So, I know I warned you that I was kind of wild...
And spontaneous.

But when I say the book fell off the shelf—it was like it **JUMPED**, and when I read those words, I realized I wanted to find God too—and I was willing to **GO ANYWHERE** to do it.

So, I decided I would go to India, and I would ask everyone I met if they could help me find God

(I told you I could be a 100 percent certified Grade-A Let's-Go-For-It-No-Matter-How-Crazy-It-Sounds Guy. You can call it one of my special skills ...)

and no matter where they sent me, **I WOULD SAY YES.**

'YES'—NO MATTER WHAT

When they told me to swim in the Ganges, I would say YES.

When they told me to hike to the mountaintop, I would say YES.

When they told me to make a ton (no, really, a literal TON) of rice, I would say YES.

When they told me to forget who I was and embrace only love, I would say YES.

So, even though the adventure terrified me, that's what I did.

I spent two months in India
on a God-seeking mission.*

*A REALLY BRIEF DEFINITION OF GOD
(like the briefest definition ever):
God is whatever you think God is.

I wanted to find out **what I thought God was.**

I met with gurus
    and priests
        and Buddhist monks
            and regular people
              and leaders
                and followers.

I swam in the Ganges and hiked to a mountaintop.
And the whole time, I just kept saying *yes*.

Because **YES** is the one of the most powerful
words in the English language.

It means, **I AM HERE.**

It leads us into adventures. It forces us to be brave.

By saying **YES**, we are accepting the **MISSION** to
be **HUMAN**.

We are saying, to that vulnerable part inside each
of us, that I see you, and you matter, and I am going
to listen to you.

We are saying that, although going out there, and living the lives we want, and falling in love, and showing up for people, and getting out of ourselves...
    Can be hard and scary and painful,
        it also reminds us of *what it means to be human*. To be delicately attuned to the deepest magnificence within us. To the gold that lives inside of us.

Right now.

THE EIGHT RULES OF YES

1 Saying yes opens us up to great adventures.

2 Saying yes opens us up to the unknown.

3 Saying yes shows us how to take care of each other.

4 Saying yes shows us how to take care of ourselves.

5 Saying yes builds trust.

6 Saying yes builds faith.

7 Saying yes is the language of every God.

8 Saying yes is the heart of every human.

Because when you say **YES**,
  you are opening the door to
  the greatest adventures.

But you are also opening the door to the unknown...

YES IS THE JOURNEY.

And humans are petrified of the unknown. Maybe that is why we have allowed ourselves to forget who we truly are. We would rather go through life sailing along the superficial surface than dive into the dark trenches of our own subconscious.

We have forgotten just how deep we go.

The point of this journal is to help us **REMEMBER WHO WE ARE** by touching the places in our souls and our hearts that have become lost to our consciousness.

Find those places—
    feel those places—
        by being brave,
            and you will find yourself.

Remember those days, back when we were cave people? I know it's been some time, but our brains still remember . . .
    If we left our cave at night, a lion could eat us.
    (And sometimes, they did.)
  If we went to a neighboring village, we might be killed. (Sounds about as scary as it was.)

The unknown *is* terrifying, but guess what?
    So is living a life in a box, a box created by
    our *fear* of the unknown.
A life stunted by safety.
A life that is far from the best version we can live.
Because if we aren't truly alive for it, we are asleep.

WHEN WE SAY YES, WE WAKE UP.

We wake up to what's possible.
    We wake up to our fullest potential.
        We wake up to meeting
        ourselves for the very first time.

And by saying yes, we cross an invisible threshold and tap into our greatest magnificence.

As Joseph Campbell once wrote:

"THE BIG QUESTION IS WHETHER YOU ARE GOING TO BE ABLE TO SAY A HEARTY YES TO YOUR ADVENTURE."

Faith is the **HEARTY YES**.

Not just to the outside adventures,
    not just to India
        or to Indiana,
but to the biggest adventure of all...

    It's saying yes to going inside.

And s l o w i n g down.

And finding those deep and quiet places inside that feel like God—whatever and whoever and whichever that means to you.

During my God-seeking adventure in India, there were lots of times when I wanted to go home.

Lots.

I wanted to say no.

I want to go back to my empty house
    and my loneliness
        and my depression,

but the *yes* kept pulling me along.
Thank God!

The yes _guided_ me to God, except it wasn't the kind
that you find in church or on a cross
(although those Gods are cool, too).

God wasn't at all what I expected.
God was the great, unfathomable
love between humans.
God was the energy flowing through us all.
God was the generosity offered to me
by so many people on the trip.
God was simply saying **YES** to **LIFE** even
when **LIFE** was **HARD**.

Even when I wanted to say no.

It was the moment when I wanted to go home and,
instead, ended up working in one of the biggest
kitchens on the planet: at the Golden Temple, where
they feed over 100,000 people a day. And as I
stood there in the boiling heat, making a literal ton
of rice in a steaming vat, I realized that *yes* had led
me into every great understanding of this world.

Time and time again, saying YES has led me out
of depression or fear or anxiety or the hard places
that are very much also
PART OF BEING HUMAN ...

And back out into the world.

TREASURE HUNT FOR YES

This week, see where you can say yes.
In fact, collect five yes's throughout the week:

1 If someone asks for your help, say yes.

2 If someone invites you on an adventure, say yes.

3 If someone offers you a challenge, say yes.

4 If someone asks you for your trust, say yes.

5 If someone invites you to go to India with them to find God, say yes.

Let's go back to the treasure chest . . .

On a piece of paper, or in the treasure chest on the next page, write down the five things you said yes to over the past week:

Was it to spending time with someone?
    Was it to going somewhere new?
Was it to trusting someone?
    Was it to having more faith?
Was it to having fun?

Add your "yes list" to your treasure chest. Because even when it's scary, saying yes is another hidden treasure, just waiting for you to find it.

ADVENTURE

LOVE

KINDNESS

BRAVERY

HAPPINESS

(Good things that everyone wants and would happily say yes to except it's also really hard to say yes to **GOOD THINGS**.)

(You just have to **SAY YES** to them.)

A STORY OF NOT SAYING YES

As a kid, I always wanted to be a soccer player.

It was my dream.

I was seventeen, and my teacher told me
that he could get me a scholarship at an
American university to play soccer.
I would have gone to championships.
I might have even won those championships.
I might have gone on to play soccer as a career.

But I said **NO**. And there went my dream.

Eleven years later, I was twenty-eight.
I wasn't living my dream.
I wasn't even living my own life.

But I decided to say **YES** to **ANOTHER LIFE**.
I left on a motorcycle.
I went to see the world.
I even played an enormous amount
of soccer in places like
India,
Thailand,
France,
Florida.

I met incredible people and
    found a new dream
        because I said **YES**.

Yes changed me
    because it made me my best self.

Yes changed me
    because it opened up new doors
    and ideas and worlds.

Yes changed me
    because it brought me closer to
    my understanding of God.

Yes changed me
    because it became easier for me
    to KEEP SAYING YES!

Yes changed me
    because it allowed me to
    become **ME**. The REAL ME.

Yes changed me
    because it showed me the
    MAGNIFICENCE of life.

So, think back on this week.

Where did you **SAY YES**?
    Did it begin to show you another way to live?
        Another way to be you?

Because the more we practice **YES** and the better
we get at using it,

   the more we begin to **TAP INTO**
   the great big **YES** inside.

      The place that some people call intuition ...

The voice inside of us that,
if we listen to it enough times,
   will guide us to where we need to go.

It will tell us when **NO** is the wrong answer,
   and **YES** is the right answer.

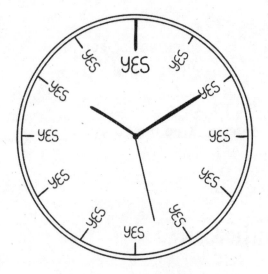

'YES'- ALL DAY, EVERYDAY

It will whisper, "This is your dream."

That voice exists within **EACH AND EVERY HUMAN BEING.**

It may have become lost to us because of technology and conditioning and society.

But it's <u>NOT lost forever.</u>

When we get **RECONNECTED** to that voice inside,
we get closer than we ever have been
to what it truly means to be human.

Intuition is our innate human capacity to connect
BEYOND the mind.
Beyond language.
To connect to who we truly are.
And the MAGNIFICENT LIFE waiting for us all.
(You included.)

MAGNIFICENT MEDAL OF BRAVERY:

YES IS THE LANGUAGE OF FAITH. THE MORE I USE IT, THE MORE FLUENT I WILL BECOME, AND THE MORE THE WORLD WILL SAY YES TO ME IN REPLY. I SAID YES!

ADVENTURE #15

**BRAVERY
IS SAYING NO**

Okay, *great*, now that you've learned to say yes, it's time to start practicing the other great brave word...

No.

WHAT, LEON? ENOUGH MADNESS...
YOU WERE JUST TELLING
ME TO SAY YES.
NOW YOU WANT ME TO SAY NO?

Precisely.

Because here is the funny thing about living a **MAGNIFICENT LIFE**:

You have to know when to take the adventure...
But you also have to know when to
PROTECT YOURSELF.

We have seen throughout history when **NO** led to great and powerful change...

Rosa Parks said **NO** when she refused to move to the back of the **BUS** and helped push the Civil Rights Movement forward.

Nelson Mandela said **NO** to hate when he was released from prison after twenty-seven years and went on to lead a free nation.

Mother Teresa said **NO** to money and greed and saved thousands of people through her charitable works.

No isn't about denying others their power; **NO** is about proclaiming our **OWN**.

HERE ARE THE EIGHT RULES OF NO:

1 Saying no helps us to understand what we don't want.

2 Saying no helps us to know what we *do* want.

3 Saying no shows people how much we value ourselves.

4 Saying no helps teach others to value us.

5 Saying no shows the world and ourselves that we put ourselves first (and we should totally put ourselves first).

6 Saying no helps us better show up for others and the world around us.

7 Saying no means that we aren't willing to hide ourselves.

8 Saying no shows the world who we are.

As with *yes*, saying *no* helps us tap into our intuition and leads us to the truest version of ourselves.

HOW CAN YOU START TO SAY NO?

Think of the one area where you need to start setting boundaries—real, tangible, ironclad boundaries. It could be at work or with friendships or romance or family. Wherever it is, it's time to put your no's into action. But first, you need to put your no's into words.

But FIRST, we have to find the no's inside us. Sometimes there are parts of us that are

SCREAMING "no" and sometimes the "no" is so quiet, it's a whisper.

Sometimes we need to say no to a person in our life—a parent or a sibling, a friend or a girlfriend, someone we work with or go to school with . . .

> Sometimes we have to say no to something that is being asked of us— we're being asked to do too much or be too much or be someone we're not . . .

Sometimes we have to say no to ourselves—when we keep making the same choice over and over, expecting a different outcome.

We need to get **REAL QUIET** in order to hear our NO's

> and to start practicing them.

It's time for the
NO DIARY (PART ONE)*

*No Diary Disclaimer: We all have places in our lives where we need to start saying "no" more. It could be to a certain person or it could be in a work or school situation. Where in your life do you need to start putting yourself first—or where do you need to start saying **NO** now?

When we say no, we're actually saying,

"THIS IS WHO I AM, AND THIS IS HOW I DESERVE TO BE TREATED."

But <u>not</u> just by other people.

Sometimes *we're* the ones we need to say no to.

Because it's not just about saying no to other people,

but also saying no to choices, habits,
or behaviors in our life that we're
responsible for changing.

NO DIARY (PART TWO)

Do you need to create boundaries
around your social media?
Do you need to slow down on
any unhealthy behaviors
or make better choices for your life?

Do you need to stand up for yourself
(we'll practice more of this later—but
you can still do it **RIGHT NOW**)?

What do you want to let into your life?

And what do you want to keep out?

What do you need to start cutting
out or cutting down in your life?

Do you need to say no to chocolate or alcohol?

Do you need to start saying no to spending
too much money or shopping online?

What habit do you need to start saying **NO** to?

Because here is the not-so-secret secret about no:

No is one of the hardest words in the human language to say.

So, start practicing it **RIGHT NOW**.

Say **NO** out loud.

Like, really loud.

NO

SAY IT LOUD (LIKE REALLY LOUD)

Say it in a WHISPER.

Say it with all the

STRENGTH

inside you.

Say it until you get comfortable with how it sounds coming out of your mouth...

NO! Nee

NON!

Nein Na

OCHI!

(This last one is Greek because, just in case my last name didn't give it away, I'm Greek, too!)

Ultimately, saying no is how we say, *this is how I want to live my life,* and *this is how I* **NO LONGER WILL**.

How can you start using no to guide you through— and to—the life you want?

How can no be your flashlight in the dark, showing you what you want by showing you what you *don't* want?

Because we can't appreciate the light until we embrace the shadows,

understanding the parts of ourselves that are willing to take less than we deserve,

that are willing to sacrifice parts of ourselves,
    our dreams,
        our humanity,
            in order to make others happy,
        even if it's at the sake of our own happiness.

Now, it's time to take all those NO's and **PUT THEM INTO ACTION**.

Look back at part one of your No Diary on page 209 and choose three areas where you're going to start saying NO today. Practice your NO in the mirror if you have to, and then get out there and **JUST SAY NO**.

THE NO PILE

YES LEON, I WILL SAY NO!

MAGNIFICENT MEDAL OF BRAVERY:

"NO" IS THE MOST POWERFUL WORD IN THE ENGLISH LANGUAGE. I DON'T HAVE TO SAY IT ALL THE TIME, BUT AS I LEARN WHEN IT'S TIME TO SAY IT, I AM FINDING THE GREAT POWER OF LIVING OUT MY MAGNIFICENCE IN EVERY CHOICE, AND IN EVERY RELATIONSHIP. NO! THERE YOU GO, I SAID IT. AGAIN.

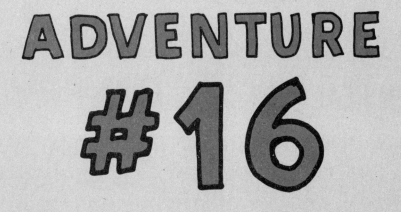

ADVENTURE #16

THE GAME OF HUMAN CONNECTION

We're going to play a game you've probably never heard of.

The good news is, it's a game any of us can play.

You can do it online or you can do it **IN REAL LIFE**.

But guess where you're going to get the most points...?

IN REAL LIFE!

Over the course of one day, you're going to connect with as many strangers as you can...

Invite your **BRAVERY BUDDY** to play along! See how many points you can earn, and who will be the ultimate winner (although winning is only a very small part of it)...

THE GAME OF HUMAN CONNECTION (IT'S ACTUALLY FUN!)*

*Game of Human Connection Disclaimer: Winning this game comes with no prizes, awards, trophies, ticker tape parades, ribbon cutting ceremonies, or one of those really big cardboard checks. It does, however, help you to live a more fearless, wiser, and truly magnificent life. And hey, if you have some ticker tape laying around, I'm here for the parade!

Reach out to a total stranger.

Don't just say hi.

MAKING FRIENDS (SORT OF)

Ask them a question. But not just any question—
Ask them . . .
   WHAT DO YOU WANT MOST IN LIFE? (5 points)
   And then **TELL THEM WHAT YOU WANT MOST IN LIFE.** (10 points—woah!)

   (If you do it online, it's half the points of doing it IRL!)

You can tell them that some guy named Leon (who is quite unsuccessfully masquerading as a Navy SEAL ...) told you to do it.

You can tell them it's for a journal on bravery.

> You can tell them that in order to be brave ...
> We have to be willing to connect.
> We have to be willing to share our dreams.

You can tell them that the more strangers you connect with in a day,
> the more points you earn,
>> and if you earn the most points,
>> **YOU WIN THE GAME OF HUMAN CONNECTION!**

And, instead of worrying about *not* winning any prizes, what you *can* do, is share your connection ...

Take a picture with your new stranger-friend if they're open to it,
> post it to social media
> (again, only if they're open to it), and
>> let me know their response.
>>> And tell us about yours.

I know this is a tough adventure to do
(BUT DO IT ANYWAY!).

Going up to a stranger and talking to them
    can be scary...
And asking them a big question can be even scarier.

But if we want to find out what it means to be
TRULY brave, we have to be willing to do SCARY
things ... including talking to a stranger.

We're so used to ignoring each other
    that we forget that seeing each other
        is what makes us **REMEMBER OURSELVES**.

When we share our dreams with each other,
we find out that the hardest parts of being human
can be healed by dreaming together.

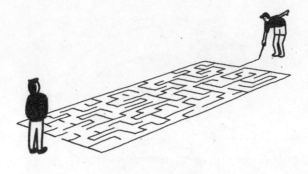

DON'T COMPLICATE
CONNECTIONS

Once you've finished playing the game, add up your
points and then see how your Bravery Buddy did ...
    What did it teach you and your Bravery Buddy
    about yourselves and your own dreams?

How did sharing your dream connect you more deeply with a stranger's dream?

How did it help turn a stranger into a friend?

Maybe this conversation happens over dinner, winner's treat—

just don't forget to let me know.

Add the hashtags #TheGameOfHumanConnection and #GoBeBrave and tag me too!

We can only find our great magnificence inside when we are willing to connect with each other.

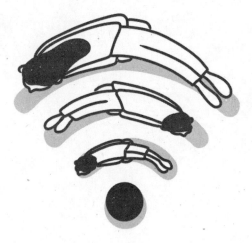

` HUMAN - F_I ` CONNECTION

MAGNIFICENT MEDAL OF BRAVERY:

WHEN WE'RE BRAVE ENOUGH TO SHARE OUR DREAMS WITH OTHERS, CONNECTION TURNS INTO RECOGNITION. I GET TO SEE THE VISION FOR MY LIFE REFLECTED IN SOMEONE ELSE'S HOPES AND DREAMS, AND I BEGIN TO SEE WHAT CAN BE. AND WHAT I SEE IS TRULY MAGNIFICENT☺.

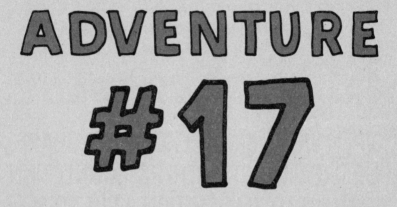

ADVENTURE #17

BURN YOUR SHIPS

I have been on a lot of adventures.

I KNOW LEON, YOU KEEP TELLING US.

I have traveled to over one hundred countries.

THIS, WE DIDN'T KNOW!,

I have driven across the world on a
little yellow motorbike,
and I have driven from the top of Alaska to the
bottom of Argentina in a little yellow bug. I've
driven from London to Mongolia, walked from the
Eiffel Tower in Paris to the Red Square in Moscow.
And probably the craziest adventure of all:
I once walked from the Los Angeles
International Airport to my house,
six and a half hours away! Long story . . .

The point is, I have done crazy things and amazing
things and incredibly stupid things.

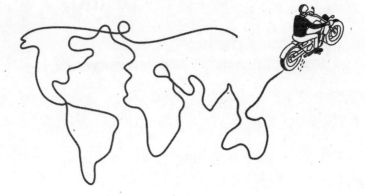

ADVENTURING ALL OVER THE WORLD

And every time, before every adventure,

I experience sheer and unavoidable fear.

A LITTLE BIT OF HISTORY

Historians say that when the conquistadors reached "new" and foreign lands, they would intentionally sink their own ships. They did this because they knew that, unless they got rid of the safety net that their ships represented, everyone on board would be tempted to give in to fear, and jump back on board to sail away. Instead, by scuttling the ships (the fancy term for sinking), they were forced to confront whatever unknowns lay ahead. They had to move forward in their journey.

Now . . .

Setting aside the horrible tales of
the conquistadors . . .
Sometimes we all have to find ways
to scuttle our ships.

We have to figure out how to not only overcome fear, but to embrace it.

We have to give ourselves no option but to go through with the plan.

For me, I discovered an incredibly clever and completely unrealistic way to do that: I brought along a camera crew.

From my first trip, I knew I wanted to film these adventures, to show people what the world— the *whole* world—looked like. But I also knew that if I had hired an entire film crew to join me, I couldn't turn around and not do it.

By facing that fear, by tricking my mind, I transmuted my fear into gold.

Because here is the funny thing about fear: often when we feel it the most, it's because we're **SO CLOSE** to the adventure we're supposed to have.

An arrow cannot move forward without first being drawn back.

The fear is actually a deep knowing that we are about to receive a gift, but because we don't know what that gift is, we become terrified.

Embracing fear is one of the
bravest things we can do—
     and one of the most human.

Ready to embrace yours?

BECAUSE IT'S TIME TO BURN YOUR SHIPS.

BURN YOUR SHIPS

(For those of you who actually have a ship, please do
not actually go and burn it! That would be terrible—
and also, YOU HAVE A SHIP?!)

What is the one thing you have been afraid to do?

THE ONE THING THAT YOU NEED TO DO IN ORDER TO HAVE A MAGNIFICENT LIFE.

YOUR GREATEST BURIED TREASURE—THE ULTIMATE VULNERABLE PLACE.

YOUR BIG TRUTH.

Is it that you want to be promoted?
Do you need to stand up to your family?
Do you need to quit your job?
Is it asking someone out on a date?
Is it breaking up with someone?

Is it asking for a film crew to follow you around as you travel the world on the kindness of strangers even though you have no idea what you're actually doing?

What is the one great truth you need to share?

What is the one great unknown you need to conquer?

And how can you do that without looking back?

Bravery is allowing ourselves to experience fear. It's about overcoming our fears in order to embark on the greatest adventure of all—our lives. As the pastor Mark Batterson once said:

THERE ARE MOMENTS IN LIFE WHEN WE NEED TO BURN THE SHIPS TO OUR PAST. WE DO SO BY MAKING A DEFINING DECISION THAT WILL ELIMINATE THE POSSIBILITY OF SAILING BACK TO THE OLD WORLD WE LEFT BEHIND. YOU BURN THE SHIPS NAMED *PAST FAILURE* AND *PAST SUCCESS*. YOU BURN THE SHIP NAMED *BAD HABIT*. YOU BURN THE SHIP NAMED *REGRET*. YOU BURN THE SHIP NAMED *GUILT*. YOU BURN THE SHIP NAMED *MY OLD WAY OF LIFE*.

Let's go back to our treasure chest. You can use your physical treasure chest or the one I've provided on the next page.

Either way, it's time to write down YOUR BIG TRUTH.

The one thing you need to do.
The. One. Thing. You. Absolutely. Must. Do.

Write it down. Now.
(*Thanks so very much, indeed.*)

In order to build your magnificent life (which you *are* building, like, **RIGHT NOW AS YOU DO THIS JOURNAL**), we sometimes have to leave the OLD ONE behind.

LEAVING YOUR OLD SELF BEHIND

You don't have to physically <u>do it</u> right now. (Spoiler alert: don't worry, by the end of the journal you actually **WILL** be doing it!)

For now,
take some time,
think about it…

But start envisioning what your life would be like if you burned your ships.

(And again, not your real ships—or anything else for that matter. We are metaphorically burning things here, okay? <u>METAPHORICALLY</u> ☺.)

What decision could forever change your life and help you to begin building a new one?

And then send it to me.

You can email me at Leon@GoBeBraveBook.com.

I'm happy to hold you accountable.
I'll stand with you next to the fire.
In fact, we can make s'mores.

By sharing your **BIG TRUTH**,
you have become accountable, and
now there's no going back...

MAGNIFICENT MEDAL OF BRAVERY:

BURNING MY SHIPS ISN'T JUST SOME CRAZY THING THE CONQUISTADORS DID; IT'S A CHOICE TO COMMIT TO THE FUTURE I DESERVE. ONCE I REALIZE THAT THE LIFE I AM BUILDING IS JUST TOO GOOD TO GIVE UP, THERE IS NO WAY I CAN GO BACK TO THE ONE I HAD. I BURNT ALL MY SHIPS, LEON! OKAY, ONLY ONE OF THEM, BUT IT'S STILL PRETTY EPIC!

ADVENTURE #18

STAND UP FOR WHAT'S RIGHT

ANOTHER TALE OF INDIA

In 2010, I went to India.

It wasn't my first time, and it wouldn't be my last time.

INCREDIBLE INDIA !

I always say, if you really want to find yourself, go to India.

Not because you will meet some amazing guru who will show you the way (although that might happen too), but because you will be faced with humanity in all its guises—the brilliant, the incredible, the hard, and the desperate.

You will see things you never knew were possible, and not just because it's a magical place
(though it can be),
    but because it is so deeply human.

It is the reminder of everything we are.
    With every blaring horn,
        with every blazing fire,
            with every heavy breath,
                and with every warm breeze.

It is every color and sound and emotion and flavor of the human experience,
    of this strange and magnificent moment
    where we get to exist here on Earth.

And on that trip in 2010 I saw what it means to stand up for that human experience, even under some of the toughest conditions. Because I met Chinarasu.

Chinarasu is a modest man living in the Bihar state, which, at the time, was one of the most dangerous places in India. Gangs roamed the towns and people were often beaten for no reason. And worse. I was honestly terrified to go there, but the guide who brought me to India insisted we visit Chinarasu, who had been one of Gandhi's disciples. Yeah, that Gandhi.

Chinarasu grew up in Bihar and he could have moved to any other province in India, but he stayed home after India won its independence from Britain to be with his people.

The gangs protected him as he walked and lived and worked among some of the most impoverished people in the world.

He lived with them and he loved them and, ultimately, he stood up for them simply by staying there.

He opened eye and ear clinics, he helped his people despite the dangers, and he stood by them.

It takes a lot of courage to stand up for your community, especially when other people are working to tear it down.

But before we can stand up for anyone else, we have to learn to stand up for ourselves.

Chinarasu learned from Gandhi the principles of nonviolence—but he also learned that there is something even more dangerous than physical violence:

He learned the thing we have to avoid the most is passive violence* . . .

The kind that separates humans from each other every day.

*Definition: Passive violence is when we consciously ignore each other, or when our emotional needs are being ignored by others.

PASSIVE VIOLENCE

Look, we all know how easy it is to dismiss the passive violence in our lives,
the ways people, sometimes unintentionally,
    sometimes intentionally,
        make us feel less than, or not deserving
        of love and care.

And sometimes, it can be really scary to stand up for ourselves in those moments.
    To say, "No, I deserve more than this and
    I need you to treat me better."

Because Gandhi didn't recognize the opposite of violence as peace, he referred to it as **AHIMSA**, which was more than nonviolence; **IT WAS LOVE.**

When we stand up for ourselves, we are actually offering the greatest expression of love.

We are like Chinarasu.

And we can all stand up *for* love.

   We can all stand up *with* love.

We begin to see the passive violence that takes place every day—
   in our workplaces,
   on the streets,
   in stores,
   everywhere we go—
   and we begin to realize that when we ignore it,
   we are only part of it.

We begin to see that ahimsa isn't just about standing up for what's right, but about expressing our love for all humanity. Because we all deserve love and peace.

We all deserve ahimsa.

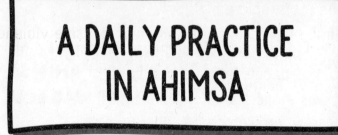

A DAILY PRACTICE IN AHIMSA

For the next week, see where you can practice ahimsa every day.

AHIMSA

Where can you stand up for yourself?

Where can you stand up for others?

Is there something you can do to stand up for your community?

Maybe it's simply a kind act,
or maybe it's calling out an act of passive violence,
saying something when someone else's emotions or
needs are being ignored.

Because when we are living in ahimsa,
we are connecting into the best version of
ourselves—the place within us that is **BRAVE**,
    that is **WILLING** to **FIGHT**,
    but not with violence,
    but with a love that **CANNOT BE SHAKEN**.

EVERYDAY AHIMSA

Ahimsa is the celebration of this human experience,
    of every color and sound and emotion and
    flavor of this brief but incredible moment that
    we get to experience here on Planet Earth.

    And that Earth not only deserves
    us standing up for it,

        it requires it.

But like all practices, let's start with ourselves.

I know, I know. Sometimes it's easier to stand up for others, but until we can begin to show ourselves ahimsa, how can we offer it to anyone else?

So, you ready?
(I know you are.)

Every day for the next week, find a way to stand up, one small act at a time.

ONE small act every day.
You can be standing up for yourself,
     you can be standing up for others,
          you can be standing up for your community.

Keep a running tally all week of all the times you stand up for something.

     See how you can do more each day.
          See how often the world gives us the
          opportunity to stand up for each other,
     if only we're willing to take it.

This isn't a competition you can win. There is no trophy (although I love trophies). What you will receive back from this practice is far more valuable: your humanity. Your flow. Your self-respect. Your dignity. Your **POWER**.

As with all these missions, your act of bravery can change the world.

By the end of the week, you will be standing up to the corner bully!

You might not yet be Gandhi, but you WILL MAKE GANDHI PROUD.

We usually know the difference between right and wrong. We know in our hearts and our guts when we are working from a place of love and when we are working from a place of anger or fear or even hate.

But it's easy to slip behind that mask of fear. It's easier to stay silent than to stand up and say, **"WE HAVE TO DO IT ANOTHER WAY."**

It's easier for someone else to save the day.

WELL, LOOK WHO JUST SHOWED UP: your Navy SEAL who doesn't really know what a Navy SEAL does, but he does know how to make you run sprints, and no one wants to have to run sprints, do they? I didn't think so.

So how about instead of waiting for someone else to step up, you think of it another way . . .

WHY NOT YOU?

Why.
Not.
You?

It takes **BRAVERY** to stand up for the **TRUTH**, but guess what?

YOU ARE BRAVE.

You're so brave, you bought a journal about it.
(I will say that once again.
And I will say it rather loudly.)

YOU. ARE. BRAVE.

MAGNIFICENT MEDAL OF BRAVERY:

STANDING UP FOR THE WORLD IS ONE OF THE MOST IMPORTANT AND SCARY CHOICES WE CAN MAKE. BUT WITHOUT OUR VOICES, THE WORLD BECOMES SILENT. I HAVE SO MUCH POWER TO SHARE, AND THE WORLD NEEDS ME NOW MORE THAN EVER. I AM READY!

ADVENTURE
#19

SELF-PORTRAIT

Ah, yes, my friend, I hope by now you've begun to realize what being brave really means:

BRAVERY IS BEING CURIOUS.

BRAVERY IS BEING PRESENT.

BRAVERY IS FALLING IN LOVE.

BRAVERY IS BEING CONNECTED.

BRAVERY IS SAYING YES.

BRAVERY IS SAYING NO.

BRAVERY IS BEING HUMAN.

BRAVERY IS BEING YOU (AND DISCOVERING ALL OF THAT HIDDEN MAGNIFICENCE INSIDE OF YOU).

BRAVERY IS SHARING YOUR GOLD.

Again, a dog knows he or she is a dog, but we humans, well, we're a trickier sort.

We forget what it means to be human.

We forget what happens when we step into our humanity and truly see each other.

We forget how brave we can really be.

WE FORGET WHO WE ARE. Because we forget *where* to find ourselves ...

I hope by now, you have begun to remember ...
   After all, you have discovered how
   to give to the people in your world ...

HOW TO LOVE
HOW TO HELP
HOW TO CONNECT

And how to say **YES** to the adventure.

It's time to say **YES** again.

It's time to take a look in the mirror and **SEE WHO YOU HAVE BECOME**.

It's time to pull out your magic markers.

And remember,

they are magic

because what you draw here is

more than a picture;

it is a poem.

CLOSE YOUR EYES, AND WITH YOUR NON-DOMINANT HAND*

(*QUICK DEFINITION: Non-dominant means if you're left-handed, use your right hand. If you're right-handed, then use your left),

DRAW YOUR SELF-PORTRAIT.

Awesome—now look at that image.

Don't look at it with judgment.
    It's not supposed to look like "you."
        It's not supposed to be "good."
            It's not supposed to be "art."

But then again, art is subjective, and if you ask me, it doesn't matter what your self-portrait looks like, it's a masterpiece just because it's you.

So, look at your picture again, and ask yourself: "Who is that person?"
    And how have they changed over the
    course of the adventures in this journal?
        How have they become more curious?
            Become more in tune with the
            magic within themselves?
        Become more present?
    Become more in love?
Become more connected?
Become more connected to their humanity?

How have they begun to build their
MAGNIFICENT LIFE?

Because you deserve a magnificent life. And if anyone tells you otherwise, send them to the very kind (fake) Navy SEAL, who will not so kindly tell them how very wrong they are.*

But now, turn to that self-portrait.
Look at the person you drew.
    No judgment, only *love*, only *awe*,
    only the *wonder* that you
saw something in yourself that you
haven't been able to see for
    a long, long time. That you haven't
    been able to feel, for a very long time.

Now, offer that portrait as
your prayer to the world.

    Share it on Instagram or somewhere else on
    social media with your new commitment.

Your commitment to be BRAVE for that person—
and for the magnificence you have buried inside.

MAGNIFICENT MEDAL OF BRAVERY:

I WANT TO WAKE UP! BECAUSE NOW THAT I AM EVERYTHING I CAN BE, I AM A LIVING MANIFESTATION OF THAT GREAT AND GOLDEN LIGHT INSIDE. EVERY DAY IS A CHOICE TO DO RIGHT BY THAT PERSON IN THE MIRROR. AND I MOST DEFINITELY DESERVE IT!

ADVENTURE
#20

THE ICE CREAM DATE OF A LIFETIME

WARNING

This adventure will be hard; it will be scary. You will think, *maybe I should skip this one.* But if you skip this one, you risk missing out on the truly magnificent life I know you can now see in front of you. You are so close, and I warn you, **DO NOT GIVE UP NOW**.

So, we all have people in our lives who we are no longer **CLOSE TO** ...

    People who have **HURT US** ...

        People we have **HURT.**

Think over the people in your life who,
if they come up in your thoughts,
    you can feel them in your gut.

Now, I will say here, if there is someone who has hurt you physically or emotionally in a way that means it is not safe to connect with them,

THEY ARE NOT THE PERSON FOR THIS MISSION.

But I imagine there are others,
    people who you know you should reach out to ...
        Who you *could* reach out to ...?
           Who would pick up the phone.
    You might be able to see what's coming here.

It's time to **MAKE PEACE**.

A LITTLE STORY ABOUT MAKING PEACE

I used to work with a friend of mine. We'll call her Tracy. Tracy and I worked together for years. She helped me to build my business. And I helped her to build hers.

But things go wrong sometimes in business.
And things went wrong between Tracy and me.
We both walked away from our time together hurt. We both felt like we had been used,

and betrayed.

And for a long time, we didn't talk to each other

Even though we had started out as friends,
now, we had nothing but bad words for each other and hurt feelings.

But here is the thing about time:
it doesn't make us forget,

but after long enough, it does begin to make us wonder, *Can we forgive?*

And sometimes that answer is **NO**, and we know it, and that's okay.

But other times, we know that the only way to find out if we can forgive is to see that person face-to-face and try to **MAKE PEACE**.

So, after a year, I called Tracy and I didn't know what else to say, so I invited her out to have (wait for it) . . . **ICE CREAM**.

She was shocked that I had called, but who can say **NO** to ice cream?

MELTING HEARTS

Tracy couldn't, and so we met.

Before we even sat down, Tracy apologized for what she had done and I apologized for what I had done, and though we knew we didn't have to be friends at the end of it, we had found something just as important.

WE FOUND FORGIVENESS.

And ice cream—because again, who can say no to ice cream?

You know what's coming next, right? I mean, I'm sure this is no surprise.

You're going to try this adventure yourself.

THE ICE CREAM DATE OF A LIFETIME*

*Any kind of ice cream variation is fine—gelato, dairy free, vegan, froyo. It's the peace that really matters.

Who is your Tracy? Pick one person who you have been wanting to reach out to . . .

Someone who **HURT YOU**,
someone **YOU HURT**.

Again, make sure it is someone who is safe for you to meet.

Someone who you know has
been waiting for the call,
   who has maybe even been wanting to call you.

And then ask them one simple question,

DO YOU WANT TO GO GET SOME ICE CREAM?

Don't say I didn't warn you; this is a hard one.

It's scary,
      and yes, that person could say no,
         they could laugh at you,
            or hang up on you.
They could reject you.

But remember, you have learned how to be **BRAVE**
      and **COURAGEOUS**
         and **WISE**
            and **LIVE A MAGNIFICENT LIFE.**

And part of living that life to its full
potential is making peace with the people
who deserve your forgiveness,
      or from whom you deserve forgiveness.

Okay, you ready? I'm right here with you. Let's pick
up the phone, pull up their number,
      and then get ready for them to answer.

EXCHANGING LOVE

Get ready to ask them that one simple question,
and then make the plan, go get ice cream,
and experience one of the biggest lessons
of this great **HUMAN EXPERIENCE**:

WE.
NEED.
EACH.
OTHER.

And that is the most profound
yet simple truth there is.
It isn't just a brave act to forgive. It is a human one.
Because we *do* need each other.

And I can promise you,
right now,
at this exact moment,
someone is waiting for your call.

So, who is that person?

Make the call,
make the ice cream date of a lifetime.
Make the **PEACE**.

And then let me know what happened,
or call your Bravery Buddy.

Not every story is tied up with a
ribbon or with a cherry on top.

Even if your person said no or the conversation
was hard or something was weird,
the fact that you reached out your hand and
even EXTENDED an ice cream invitation
is one of the bravest actions you could have taken.

And if things didn't go perfectly
(or even all that great),
that makes it even braver.

Because here's the thing about Tracy and me.
We haven't spoken since our ice cream date, and
I don't know that we ever will.

Even ice cream can't heal all wounds,
but it can help us to acknowledge them, to find
closure, to be able to move on . . .

With or without a cherry on top.

MAGNIFICENT MEDAL OF BRAVERY:

FORGIVENESS IS BEST SERVED WITH ICE CREAM. IN OFFERING FORGIVENESS, ASKING FOR IT, OR DOING BOTH, I HAVE COMMITTED ONE OF THE SWEETEST AND MOST IMPORTANT ACTS OF BEING HUMAN. AND I MUST SAY, THE ICE CREAM WAS RATHER DELICIOUS!

TAKE A BREAK

So, I have done a lot of traveling. A LOT. Like, more than most people (have I mentioned that yet?).

Anyway, what I have found is that the BIGGEST adventures happen when we **TAKE A BREAK** from the adventure.

But here's the thing: **IT'S NOT EASY TO TAKE A BREAK**.

It's a lot easier to plan and write to-do lists and run errands and watch TV and play video games ...

But not today!

Today (and by today, I mean a day where you don't have a lot of obligations—in fact, clear your schedule) it's time to **TAKE A BREAK**.

WAIT, LEON, ARE YOU TELLING ME THAT BRAVERY IS DOING NOTHING?

We're not doing nothing ...

We're **TAKING A BREAK**.

NO MORE TASKS FOR TODAY

You can leave the house or not ...
See where the day leads you.

You might decide you want to go to a museum.
You might decide you want to go for a walk.
You might decide you want to read a book.

But don't feel obligated to do anything at all.
Bravery is also about resting, about getting quiet
enough that we can hear what we really need ...

And then being willing to give that GIFT
of what we need to ourselves.

If you want to see if your Bravery Buddy wants to
join you in taking a break, great!

You can even ask one of your
friends or a family member—

you can **TAKE A BREAK** TOGETHER ...

Either way, make sure you're taking a break
effectively: turn off the TV, put away your phone
(and think about how addicted we are to our phones
that I don't even want to suggest that you don't look
at them all day), give yourself a break from all the
things we have to do and know and be.

Only then will you be able to see
all the invitations calling you.

If a bird is chirping outside, go listen to it.
If it flies away, see where you can follow it.

Follow the signs.
Wake up and let the day take you.

You don't have to run the errands ...
You don't have to fix the thing that is broken ...
You don't have to do anything but ...

GO OUT THERE AND EXPLORE.

Even for just a couple of hours,
let yourself be a kid again ...

Remember back to
summer vacations
when you were a kid,

and all you had to do
was take a break.

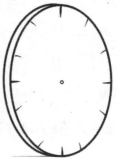

TAKE SOME TIME OUT
FOR A BREAK

In fact, there was so
much break taking
that you started
having to find adventures
wherever you could.

You went exploring and skipping stones
and making up characters
and playing soccer against yourself
(without the wall punching of course).

When we have nothing to do,
    we have the space and the time and
    the childlike excitement ...

To tap into our creativity, and find the greatest
adventure of all: the one inside ourselves.

MAGNIFICENT
MEDAL OF BRAVERY:

THERE IS NO GREATER ADVENTURE THAN
THE ONE THAT HAPPENS OUT OF BOREDOM.
I GOT TO REST, I GOT TO RECHARGE, BUT
MORE IMPORTANTLY, I GOT TO FIND
OUT JUST HOW FUNNY, SPONTANEOUS,
BRILLIANT, EXCEPTIONALLY BEAUTIFUL,
LOVING, AND WEIRD I CAN BE WHEN I HAVE
NOTHING ELSE TO DO. IT WAS ACTUALLY
RATHER FUN.

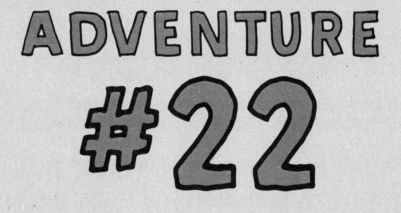

ADVENTURE #22

BUDDY SUMMIT

Okay, it's time for a very important meeting...
Maybe one of the most important
meetings of your life...

Like so important, you might want to put on a suit
and tie, or a dress, or a suit-and-tie dress.
Or just wear whatever you want
because I don't wear suits and ties...

But I *do* wear a fake Navy SEAL persona and I am here
to say in my deepest, strongest, Navy SEAL voice...

IT'S TIME TO CONVENE A WORLD-CHANGING, LIFE-ALTERING CONFERENCE OF TWO OF THE GREATEST MINDS TO EVER WALK THIS FINE EARTH ...

IT'S TIME FOR A BUDDY SUMMIT.

GREAT BRAINS COMING TOGETHER

Also, if you haven't chosen a Bravery Buddy yet—
thinking maybe I'd forget about it or you really
didn't need one—well, time to go find one.

Now.

I'll wait . . .

Because we can't **GO BE BRAVE**
by ourselves.

We need a partner in this work . . .
Especially the **BIG WORK** that we're about to do.

So, I want you to think back to Adventure #17:
BURN YOUR SHIPS.

What was the one thing you said you needed
to do in order to CHANGE YOUR LIFE . . .?

Was it quit your job? Start writing? Stand up to
your family? Break a habit? Build a new one?

WHAT WAS YOUR BIG TRUTH?

Go back to your TREASURE CHEST
on page 104 and see what it says . . .
You don't have to be ready to do it yet . . . but
don't worry, you won't be doing it alone.

That's why we're calling a **BUDDY SUMMIT**.
It's time to meet up with your Bravery Buddy. And
if you don't have one, reach out to me. I can be your
Bravery Buddy or we can create a Bravery Buddy

community, where you can all cheer each other on and play this game together!

You can go to a coffee shop or use FaceTime or get a Zoom Room (just like the United Nations!).

Hopefully, you and your Bravery Buddy have been doing some of the adventures in this journal together, so if they've already done the **BURN YOUR SHIPS** exercise, GREAT!
        If they haven't, that's okay, too—you'll just do another Buddy Summit when they're ready.

Either way, you're going to bring your journal to the coffee shop or FaceTime or Zoom Room . . . You're going to open up your TREASURE CHEST (if you've built one—and if not, turn back to page 104 to refresh yourself on your one BIG TRUTH), and you're going to tell your Bravery Buddy the one decision you need to make to . . .

FIND THAT GREAT MAGNIFICENCE INSIDE OF YOU AND **BRING IT TO THE SURFACE OF YOUR LIFE.**

And then you're going to talk about why you haven't made that decision yet . . .

BUT *REALLY* TALK ABOUT IT.

Talk about the fears, the obstacles, the desires, the dreams—all those feelings that come up when you think about this big truth.

And don't be afraid to get deep. I mean, if you're not crying by the end of the Buddy Summit, is it even a Buddy Summit?!

And then, together with your Bravery Buddy, you're going to develop a communiqué (a fancy-sounding word for an official announcement) about your plan of action to turn that Big Truth into your Big Decision— again, just like the UN.

PLAN OF ACTION

But first we're going to set up some SEAL Team rules to help us draft our communiqué. Consider them the guidelines to your mission, should you choose to accept it—but at this point in the journey, I'm afraid you're all in!

SIX RULES OF OUR SEAL TEAM:

1 Keep it simple.

2 Never assume.

3 Don't be afraid to fail.

4 Take risks.

5 Never be satisfied.

6 You don't have to like it; you just have to do it.

And as your super-not-experienced in being a Navy SEAL but super-experienced in doing scary things author, I can tell you that when you create a plan, you are HALFWAY TO ACTION.

So that's what you're going to do: you're going to write out the small steps you need to take in order to make the decision real . . .

Okay, let's take it step by step. Think about your BIG TRUTH and then ask yourself:

HOW CAN I KEEP MY BIG TRUTH SIMPLE?

_____

WHAT ARE SOME ASSUMPTIONS I'M MAKING ABOUT IT?

_____

WHAT WOULD HAPPEN IF I FAILED?

_____

WHAT IS THE REAL RISK HERE?

_____

WHAT ISN'T WORKING ABOUT MY CURRENT SITUATION?

_____

HOW CAN I MAKE SURE I GO THROUGH WITH THE BIG DECISION?

_____

What are the baby steps—or should we say, the **BUDDY STEPS**—you need to take? And which ones can you start taking today?

If your buddy is also ready to draft their official communiqué, make the time to work through their SEAL Team rules and their BUDDY STEPS, too.

See how, moving forward, you can help each other to not just **BURN YOUR SHIPS**...

But begin to **BUILD NEW ONES**.

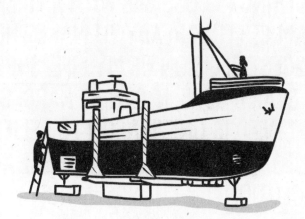

SHIP BUILDING, TOGETHER

MAGNIFICENT MEDAL OF BRAVERY:

ANYTHING IS POSSIBLE WITH A FRIEND.
I AM GETTING READY TO MAKE THE
BIGGEST DECISION OF MY LIFE. SURE,
IT'S SCARY; SURE, IT CAN BE HARD; BUT
ALL I NEED IS ONE PERSON TO BELIEVE
IN ME IN ORDER TO CREATE GREAT AND
REVOLUTIONARY CHANGE IN HOW I LIVE
MY LIFE.

I. WILL. GO. BE. BRAVE.

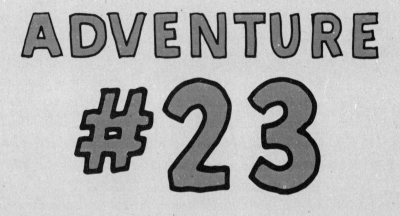

ADVENTURE #23

THE BIG DECISION

I have read nearly a thousand books. I am not kidding. This is what happens when you're bullied as a kid: **YOU READ**. A lot.

And the best books are the ones that shifted something so deep inside of me . . .

They changed who I was.

SINKING INTO THE PAGES

The ones that spoke to that broken place inside and promised me that I was going to be okay.

The ones that told me **I COULD BE WHOEVER I *WANTED* TO BE.**

I hope that this is one of those books for you.

I really, really do.

And if it hasn't been so far, I promise that if you do this final adventure, it most certainly will be.

Because remember when we talked
about burning your ships ...?

And you wrote down the one thing you need to do
in order to live your most
MAGNIFICENT LIFE
and I said you didn't need to do it right then?

Well guess what?
You get to do it <u>**RIGHT NOW**</u>.

But who are we kidding? I know you're ready by now.
You've been working towards this
VERY moment ...

YOU ARE FEARLESS
AND WISER
AND READY TO LIVE
A MAGNIFICENT LIFE.

Because I promise you, once you start living your
GVOY (remember that? Greatest Version of
You!), you won't be able to live life any other
way. You will know what it means to be **TRULY
HUMAN** and you will be **BRAVE ENOUGH** to live
from that space 23½ hours out of every day.

MEETING YOUR GREATER SELF

(It's okay, you can still be sad
or scared or bored or lonely.)
Because life is still LIFE.

SO GO BACK TO YOUR BIG TRUTH
on page 229...

The one thing that if you did it
**WITHOUT A SHADOW
OF A DOUBT,**
it would change your world.

What is the one thing you're holding onto that is
stopping you from the **LIFE** you know you deserve?

The one that is whispering to you right now. That delicate voice within that is trying to get your attention and has been trying to get your attention F O R E V E R!

If it is a conversation you need to have ...
If it is a job you need to quit ...
If it is a job you need to ask for ...
If it is a relationship you need to leave ...
Or a relationship you need to start ...

It's time to turn that Big Truth into *the* Big Decision. To turn your inner magnificence into

A MAGNIFICENT LIFE.

HOW CAN YOU ACHIEVE YOUR GREAT FINAL ACT OF BEING BRAVE?

HOW CAN YOU FIND THE GREAT ADVENTURE WAITING FOR YOU ON THE OTHER SIDE OF FEAR?

So, the Navy SEAL is back ... and he is ready to help you in your final mission:

To **BE A NAVY SEAL IN YOUR OWN LIFE.**

Not the type who runs into buildings and saves people, but the type who deeply feels their own pain and acts courageously from that place. In other words ...

SOMEONE. EXACTLY. LIKE. YOU.

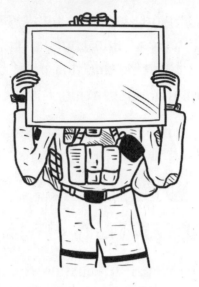

YOU ARE THE NAVY SEAL

It's like the real-life Navy SEAL shared in the retreat I went to: there is bravery on the battlefield, but the truest bravery emerges when we share **OUR TRUTHS** with each other.

AND WITH OURSELVES.

(And change our lives from that place of *inner truth*.)

It's time to take the **BRAVERY** you've been building inside of you and turn it into the **COURAGE** you need to
  do the one thing, take the first step,
    that will shift something deep inside of you . . .
      That will heal the broken place inside . . .

That will allow you to be whoever you want to be...

THAT WILL SET YOU FREE.

Now, go ahead and put the journal down...

AND GO ACTUALLY DO IT.

DO. THE. THING. THAT. WILL. CHANGE. EVERYTHING.

RIGHT NOW.

IT'S TIME!

Come back when you're done...
I'll be waiting.

THE BLANK SPACE BELOW IS TO ILLUSTRATE THE TIME YOU HAVE TAKEN TO MAKE THE PHONE CALL, SEND THE EMAIL, MEET THE PERSON, PUT THAT FIRST THING IN PLACE TO START LIFE AFRESH. DO THE THING THAT WILL FOREVER CHANGE YOUR LIFE.*

*The BIG Decision Disclaimer: I know that this might be something that will take time. We can't change everything with one phone call, email, or even meeting. But we can take the first step.

OKAY, DID YOU DO IT?
WOW—I AM SO PROUD OF YOU.

Really, if I could jump through the page and hug you (which might be a little weird for both of us), I would.

But since I can't, what I can do is tell you to take a deep breath and honor the BIG DECISION you just made.

Come here, sit down...
(Can I get you some water?)
Are you okay? How did it feel to take the first step?

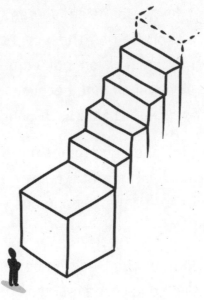

THE FIRST STEP IS THE HARDEST

To make the BIG DECISION?

Do you need to call your Bravery Buddy?

If you don't have a Bravery Buddy, remember you can always use me. Email me at Leon@ GoBeBraveBook.com. You can share your BIG DECISION on social media, or you can tell one friend, but let *somebody* reach out and HUG YOU and say . . .

WOW—I AM SO PROUD OF YOU.

By the way, I want you to know it's totally normal if, after you made the Big Decision, the whole world didn't shift on its axis right away—but also, know you're safe even if it did. I'm not here to promise you the world after you've made the Big Decision, but I am here to say that your life will change because you will have a different relationship with yourself.

Now, I totally get that you might not be ready to make the Big Decision yet. I know how hard Big Decisions can be. But that just means we have more training to do.

If you *didn't* do your Big Decision because it was too hard or you were too scared, you can use the space on the next page to write about the reasons you didn't do it. BUT that also means you have to stop reading and go back to the start.

That's right.

You get to do the journal again—congratulations!

If you *did* do it, well, HURRAY! Soon, you get to
put this journal on a shelf, tell your friends about it,
or, if you're really ready to move on, bury it in your
backyard. (But maybe don't do that—not sure how
environmentally sound of a decision that is.)

I know it's been scary at times . . .
    But everything we've done together
    throughout these adventures has led you

to this moment—the moment that we actually **MAKE THE CHANGE**.

That we realize that we get to choose how magnificent our lives will be.

And when we're brave enough to choose the lives we were always meant to live,

WE FIND THE REAL TREASURE THAT HAS BEEN WAITING FOR US THIS WHOLE TIME: THE <u>FREEDOM</u> TO BE WHO WE REALLY ARE.

The freedom to be you. The freedom to be me.

The freedom to be funny, spontaneous, brilliant, exceptionally beautiful, loving, weird HUMANS!

And the bravest thing you can do is to BE TRULY HUMAN . . . again and again and again.

Because it doesn't end here: you have to *keep* being brave, *keep* sharing your truth.

Only then can we step into our humanity and see ourselves clearly.

And when we can see ourselves in all our value, all our worth . . .

We can see it in each other, too.

When you connect to your humanity by
listening to that vulnerable place inside,
    when you feel it flowing through you,
everything that you have needed (not wanted)
will come to you in droves.

And when it comes, you will feel it
like the bird feels flight.

Like the dog feels unconditional love.

You will feel it all.

    You will feel it in the place of
    your truest humanity ...

You dove so deep that you found the buried
treasure inside of you.

But you also did the work to
bring it up to the surface,
to share it with others,
to say, *look what was there this whole time,*
and *I can't deny my truth,*
    my treasure,
        my life
            anymore.

And that is **THE GREATEST ADVENTURE OF ALL.**

And yours has **JUST BEGUN.**

MAGNIFICENT MEDAL OF BRAVERY:

WE WILL NEVER KNOW IF WE MADE THE RIGHT DECISION IF WE NEVER MAKE A DECISION AT ALL. I'VE MADE ONE OF THE BIGGEST CHOICES IN MY LIFE. I CHOSE TO BE FREE, TO BE ME, TO LIVE THE MOST MAGNIFICENT VERSION OF THIS SHORT BUT BEAUTIFUL STAY ON PLANET EARTH.

ADVENTURE
#24

YOUR
MAGNIFICENCE MAP

WHAT, LEON?

I HAVE TO KEEP GOING?

I DID THE THING.

I MADE THE BIG DECISION.

I CHOSE A MAGNIFICENT LIFE.

I GOT TO THE OTHER SIDE OF FEAR.

AND YOU'RE STILL HERE!

Well, yes, yes, I am! Sorry about that ...

But only because I'm here to give you an incredibly valuable tool that will help you on your journey to keep living your MAGNIFICENT LIFE!

YOUR MAGNIFICENCE MAP*

*Magnificence Map Disclaimer: You can make this as abstract or as realistic as you want. Your map could be a painting or a to-do list. You can do it with your non-dominant hand or the one you usually use. It could be a *Goonies*-style treasure map or it can be a five-year plan. YOUR TREASURE MAP IS *YOUR* TREASURE MAP. But ask that little kid inside, ask the bigger kid they have now become: what should my magnificent life look like?

I know what you're going to say: **Oh, NOW you're giving me the map, Leon? Aren't we supposed to start with that?**

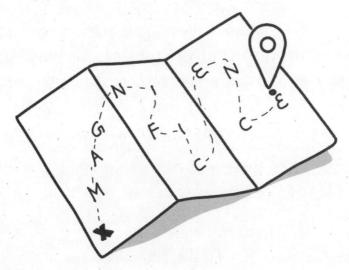

Well, not in this case ... because how are we supposed to create a map to a place we've never been before? **YOU NOW KNOW WHERE TO FIND THE BURIED TREASURE WITHIN YOURSELF.**

And you can draw a map right to it so that you never forget how to get back to the place inside where we see the funny,

    spontaneous,

        brilliant,

            exceptionally magnificent,

loving,
and weird
SPARKLING DIAMOND
we have found in ourselves.

But here's the thing—we aren't exactly experts on *treasure maps*. It's been too long since we've seen *The Goonies* and we haven't gone spelunking since we were eight. Most of us aren't exactly modern-day pirates or explorers or cartographers (or maybe you are, in which case ... that's amazing), so we don't use treasure maps on a daily basis.

But what we *can* do is ask that eight-year-old to help us draw one ...

Your little English boy or American girl—your **LITTLE YOU.**

Remember them?
They have always believed in you—
they remember every dream
you have ever had,
they know the awe and excitement
that this life deserves.

And now they are going to help you find your way back there whenever you need it.

THEY ARE GOING TO DRAW OR WRITE OR DRAW AND WRITE THE INSTRUCTIONS ON HOW TO GET TO YOUR MAGNIFICENT LIFE.

So, ask that eight-year-old:
WHAT DOES MY MAGNIFICENT LIFE LOOK LIKE?

Let your inner child tell you; let them create the vision for your future. (But if they tell you to play soccer against yourself, and then punch a wall when you lose, please don't listen!)

Let them show you what that **MAGNIFICENT LIFE** looks like.

But guess what, we're not just going to **WRITE IT**,
   or draw it,
       or to-do list it.

We're going to **CREATE IT**.

Share your MAGNIFICENCE MAP with a friend or
family member or your Bravery Buddy.

Or you can film it . . .
PERFORM YOUR MAGNIFICENT LIFE.

Show the **WORLD** the vision you have created . . .

   And invite them to share theirs.

You can make a TikTok or a Reel.
   You can keep it to yourself,
       or you can **SHARE IT WITH THE WORLD**.

You can hashtag #MagnificentLife and
#GoBeBrave; you can tag me @TheKindnessGuy.

And then take a moment to look at your **map** again,
   take it outside,
       be with that promise to yourself,
           be with the prayer.

Look at how that vision lines up with the life you are
living right now . . .

MAKE YOUR OWN JOURNEY

Where do you need **MORE**?

Not more work
or money
or followers
or consumption...

WHERE DO YOU NEED MORE OF WHAT WILL MAKE YOUR LIFE MAGNIFICENT?

(And then begin to create it.)

And if you have an actual, physical, hand-painted, hot glue-gunned TREASURE CHEST, feel free to keep your MAGNIFICENCE MAP inside it so you will always know **WHERE TO FIND IT**.

Oh, and just one final little reminder about BRAVERY:

Bravery means to find the place within that feels broken (sometimes in big ways, other times in small ones), a place we all have, and to give it hope. To find that place at the very center of our existence that needs us more than anything has ever needed us before. The place within us that is free.

So, find *that place*, always,
and then find out what it needs.

What hidden treasures do you need to still find? And what hidden magnificence is hiding inside?

If you need more kindness,
offer more kindness.
If you need more love,
offer more love.
If you need more adventure,
offer more yes's.
If you need more strength,
offer more no's.
The more we commit to our paths,
the faster we will get to where we want to go.

That doesn't mean that we won't fail or get hurt or be rejected or have **BAD THINGS HAPPEN**.

Life can be cruel.
And mean.
And hard.
And it can leave scars.
Sometimes it just leaves scabs.

BUT THE SCAB CANNOT BECOME THE SCAR UNTIL WE ARE WILLING TO HEAL.

So be brave, and do the work. I promise it's worth it. Because as your Navy SEAL would say . . .

YOU ONLY GET ONE CHANCE TO LIVE THIS LIFE.

Now GO LIVE IT.
It's time.

To **GO BE BRAVE**.

MAGNIFICENT MEDAL OF BRAVERY:

WHO KNEW BRAVERY COULD LOOK LIKE THIS (ESPECIALLY WITH SUCH A POOR IMPRESSION OF A NAVY SEAL LEADING IT)? BUT BY LEARNING TO BE BRAVE, I HAVE LEARNED HOW TO BE THE TRUEST HUMAN, THE PERSON THAT WAS ALWAYS THERE, ASKING SOMETIMES GENTLY, SOMETIMES THROUGH ANGER OR PAIN, TO BE FREED. I NOW HAVE A MAP TO MY LIBERATION: I VOW TO USE IT AT EVERY TURN.

ADVENTURE #24³⁄₄

THE HAPPY DANCE

As the great psychiatrist Viktor Frankl
wrote in his book about surviving the Holocaust,
Man's Search for Meaning:

"EVERYTHING CAN BE TAKEN FROM A MAN BUT
ONE THING: THE LAST OF THE HUMAN FREEDOMS—
TO CHOOSE ONE'S ATTITUDE IN ANY GIVEN SET OF
CIRCUMSTANCES, TO CHOOSE ONE'S OWN WAY."

We always have a choice,

even when it feels like we have no choice,
and yes, sometimes we might choose to be sad.

Because sad things happen.
　　People die,
　　　　pets die,
　　　　　　we don't get something we want,
　　　　　　　and we lose something we had.

We have every right to be sad
and upset and melancholy.

There were days in my depression where I
absolutely had to choose sadness.

　　I had to go through my grief
　　in order to get to my healing.
　　Because depression has its own path.

　　　　But you can also choose to
　　　　tell someone about your sadness,
　　　　　　to get therapeutic help,
　　　　　　　to find a solution.

And at a certain point, I had to make a different
decision for myself.

I had to choose happiness.

　　Because here is a funny thing about
　　HAPPINESS—we really only need to do
　　one thing to remind ourselves that we can
　　be HAPPY whenever we need to be.

Which is why this is the last ¾ of an adventure: because it's sort of like an oxygen tank that you can always come back to when you need some air. And it's a really simple adventure, but it still requires bravery (we don't call it **GO BE BRAVE** for nothing).

ALL YOU HAVE TO DO IS PUT ON SOME MUSIC . . .

And . . .

HAPPY DANCE.

DANCING PEOPLE ARE HAPPY PEOPLE

Yup.

As soon as you finish reading this paragraph, I don't care where you are—at home, at work, on the bus, in school, at the dentist . . .

Get some music on your phone,
    your favorite song,
        the one you know you love to dance to.

And **GUESS WHAT**?
YOU'RE GOING TO DANCE!*

*Now go throw on the song "It's Time" by Imagine Dragons and start dancing!

MAGNIFICENT MEDAL OF BRAVERY:

AT ANY GIVEN MOMENT, AT ANY GIVEN TIME, I HAVE A CHOICE: TO DANCE OR NOT TO DANCE. RIGHT THIS VERY SECOND, I AM GOING TO DANCE! BECAUSE I DESERVE IT!

ACKNOW-
LEDGMENTS

Art truly does imitate Life.

Whilst I wrote this journal for you, ultimately I also wrote it for myself. During the time I was writing it, things were not easy.

Bravery and courage were needed.

The people below believed, sometimes even when I didn't.

Each of them, in some profound way, helped create the magic that is within these pages. But most importantly, when I was down, they lifted me up, and it is because of them that you are reading these words.

It is because of them.

Kristen, once again, your magic got us to where we needed to be. Yippee!! Thank you for your fearlessness, wisdom, and true magnificence. #MagicSprinkles

Coleen, thank you for believing in the Englishman. It never goes unnoticed, and is deeply appreciated. We did it! Again.

To all my friends at BenBella, I am sorry I drove you a little mad with the creation of this journal! I hope it was worth it ... It was most definitely worth creating such a beautiful piece of art, one that hopefully will touch many lives. I appreciate all of you. Thank you for believing in me again.

Dheeraj, your illustrations have made this journal truly magnificent. You are stuck with me for many more projects. Sorry.

Téa, thank you for loving me, through thick and thin. The unicorn came to life ...

Erick, you know what you did. And it will never be forgotten.

Ramchandra, you continue to bless me with your wisdom. The *simple* life is far holier than the *egotistical* one. Thank you once again for your friendship.

Sam, you were like a magnificent shooting star, and the team at Winston Entertainment keeps you close to their hearts. Godspeed, my friend.

Mandy and Luke, your love is felt every day. Every day.

Archie, you're a good lad. Your leader Winston would be very proud of you.

Bo, the legend of Nottingham. Thank you for believing, when belief and hope was sometimes in short supply . . .

Kami, you are a pure point of light. Your mum is my best friend, and so are you.

Ini, Hamish, and Geoffrey, I love you; thank you for being my friends.

And finally, to all of those who try to break us. Thank you. You make us fearless. You make us wiser. And you lay the unbreakable foundation for us to live a truly magnificent life.

ABOUT THE AUTHOR

Leon Logothetis is a global adventurer, motivational speaker, and philanthropist. It wasn't always that way. He used to be a broker in the city of London where he felt uninspired and chronically depressed. He gave it all up for a life on the road. This radical life change was inspired by the inspirational movie The Motorcycle Diaries.

The days of living and working behind his "slab of wood" (or desk, to the layman) are well and truly over. His new passion: Finding ways for your **inner rebel** (that voice that tells you that you are worth so much more than you think) to come out and play.

Leon has visited over 100 countries and traveled to every continent. He is the star of the discovery+ series The Kindness Diaries, where he circumnavigates the globe, relying on the kindness of strangers, while giving life-changing gifts along the way.

Prior to **The Kindness Diaries**, Leon was the host of the TV series **Amazing Adventures of a Nobody,** which was broadcast across the world by National Geographic International and, over the course of three seasons, saw Leon cross America, the United Kingdom, and Europe on just 5 dollars, 5 pounds, and 5 euros a day, respectively.

Leon is no stranger to adventure. He teamed up with First Book and drove a car from London to Mongolia, raising money to buy 10,000 books for underprivileged children in America. He also drove a vintage London taxi across America, giving free cab rides to the needy and working with Classwish to bring hope back to the schools of America.

He is a motivational speaker and the creator of the podcast **Spontaneous Moments.**

Leon has documented his travels for numerous media outlets including CBS This Morning, Good Morning America, CNN, Los Angeles Times, San Francisco Chronicle, Outside, Huffington Post, Psychology Today, and the New York Times.

He is the author of four bestselling books, **Amazing Adventures of a Nobody, The Kindness Diaries, Live, Love, Explore,** and **Go Be Kind.** He lives in Los Angeles with his dog Archie.